FINE TUNING AND MAINTAINING
OO GAUGE MODELS

Nigel Burkin

THE CROWOOD PRESS

First published in 2011 by
The Crowood Press Ltd
Ramsbury, Marlborough
Wiltshire SN8 2HR

www.crowood.com

British Library Cataloguing-in-Publication Data
A catalogue record for this book is available from the British Library.

ISBN 978 1 84797 234 7

Typeset by Bookcraft Ltd, Stroud, Gloucestershire
Printed and bound in Singapore by Craft Print International Ltd

CONTENTS

INTRODUCTION 6

CHAPTER ONE: **RUNNING-IN NEW MODELS** 9

CHAPTER TWO: **FITTING FACTORY-SUPPLIED PARTS** 40

CHAPTER THREE: **LOCOMOTIVE WHEELS** 62

CHAPTER FOUR: **MECHANICAL ENHANCEMENTS** 105

CHAPTER FIVE: **SIMPLE ENHANCEMENTS** 136

CHAPTER SIX: **KEEPING THE LAYOUT RUNNING SMOOTHLY** 164

CHAPTER SEVEN: **ONGOING MAINTENANCE AND REPAIRS** 175

USEFUL ADDRESSES 190

INDEX 191

INTRODUCTION

Scale modelling covers a whole host of different disciplines including aircraft, ships, cars and military subjects. However, there is little to match railway modelling in its scope for authentic operation and the added dimension of movement and control made possible by the transmission of electrical current through the running rails to a locomotive. This concept in the hobby is quite old, but one that has seen much refinement in the development of Digital Command Control (DCC) and other refined operating systems in recent years.

It is this ability to introduce realistic operation to railway modelling in addition to the activities of building, construction and landscaping that attracts so many people to the hobby. Unfortunately, operations depend on a number of other factors. One of those is the transmission of electricity to a locomotive so it can be powered. Another is the sheer number of delicate components involved in turnout control, locomotive operation, couplings, lighting, digital sound and rolling stock. All of these rely on standards to ensure that equipment is interchangeable between layouts and careful maintenance to sustain those standards so that the equipment works reliably time after time. Without the application of reliable standards and maintenance of equipment, scale operation to match the accurate appearance of model trains would not be possible.

This book is all about achieving the best possible and reliable operation of OO gauge model railway locomotives and the layout environment they require to run.

It is possible to make simple detailing enhancements to an off-the-shelf model with minimal outlay, as demonstrated on this model of a Class 47 by ViTrains.

LEFT: The importance of wheels and how to use wheel conversion kits is covered in the book, such as those used to convert this Bachmann Class 66 locomotive to EM gauge.

BELOW: Steam locomotives such as this Hornby Southern Railway T9 are described in detail, including how its mechanism is constructed.

The objective of the techniques covered is illustrated in this photograph of two Heljan Class 33s working smoothly in multiple on my fixed home layout, and providing operation and performance that looks like that of full-size railways.

A subject little understood by modellers, especially those new to the hobby or returning after a long absence, is the matter of locomotive and layout maintenance, and it is this that will be covered in this book together with information on how to prepare models for smooth and reliable operation on the layout. Topics include how the internal workings of the model locomotive actually function, how to keep wheels clean, how to maintain the layout for reliable running and methods for preparing a brand-new model for operation with the rest of the fleet.

All of these techniques are designed to achieve the best possible results where many compromises are needed in order to make everything work smoothly. It is unfortunate that the most common causes of problems with a model railway are dirt or inadequate lubrication, and many models are returned to the model shop for warranty repair that only need routine cleaning and lubricating in order to put them back into reliable service.

With more than twenty years' experience of operating a model railway of one sort or another, I have gathered together many different techniques for keeping my models running reliably, especially those that are getting a little long in the tooth. All the techniques I use regularly on both my exhibition layouts and my fixed home layout are described within these pages. I hope they will help you to achieve the ultimate goal of an exceptional model railway because operations are a major part of why we are all involved in this fascinating hobby. I also hope that it helps modellers setting out in the hobby to avoid the common pitfalls with regard to running-in new models correctly and then looking after them properly once they're in service on the layout.

In the preparation of this book I would like to acknowledge the kind support and practical assistance with models and equipment offered by Simon Kohler of Hornby Hobbies Ltd and Dennis Lovett of Bachmann Europe Plc.

CHAPTER ONE

RUNNING-IN NEW MODELS

*Running-in turns are a
common feature of full-size
railway operations where new
locomotives or those that
have been overhauled at a
works are tested for defects.
A second locomotive may be
in attendance, and this was
the case with this turn from
Glasgow to Carlisle where
a recently overhauled Class
90 electric locomotive was
accompanied by a Class 47.
Carlisle, January 1994.*

INTRODUCTION

Railway modelling is enjoying the introduction of
new locomotive models equipped with superior
mechanisms and electronics that deliver a superb
performance unheard of even as little as ten years
ago. Fuelled by demand for better performance
and superior detailing, companies such as Hornby,
Bachmann and ViTrains are delivering standards
close or comparable to those enjoyed by modellers
in continental Europe and North America.

Yet how many modellers take the time to 'commission' their new models before placing them in
service on a layout? After all, the full-size railways
operate commissioning trials and running-in turns
for all manner of new equipment before it is placed in
service. As model locomotive mechanisms become
more sophisticated, running-in becomes more
important to identify defects, to check if the locomotive will perform satisfactorily on your layout and to
see if it needs repairs under warranty. This chapter
looks at running-in and what you might expect to
find under the bodyshell when you first take a look

inside the model. The following points are important
with regard to introducing new models to the layout
and how to achieve trouble-free operation:

- Workbench tools and equipment.
- Lubricants and cleaners.
- First inspection.
- Why instruction leaflets are important.
- Running-in techniques.
- Test running – looking for problems on the
  layout.
- What's under the body – parts and compo-
  nents explained.
- What to do when something goes wrong.

WORKBENCH TOOLS
AND EQUIPMENT

Experienced modellers gather a wide range of tools
and sundries to assist with the maintenance and
repair of locomotives and rolling stock. Running-in
tests of new models require some important materials and a selection of general modellers' tools so that

a model can be lubricated, cleaned and adjusted with the bodyshell removed from the chassis.

Some sophisticated devices are available to assist with the process of running-in a new model, including combined loco testing and rolling road units (Gaugemaster and Hornby) or simple rolling road saddles (Bachrus, DCC Concepts and N Brass Locomotives) that can be placed on track. In both cases, such devices provide static testing facilities for new and existing models.

I have the following tools and materials to hand when working on new models straight from the box:

- Jewellers' screwdriver set for use with cross-head and slotted screws.
- Fibre scratch pencil.
- Cotton buds (Q-tips).
- Cotton cloths for cleaning.
- Fine-nose pliers for making fine adjustments.
- Tweezers for picking out fluff and to hold scraps of cloth for cleaning in tight spaces.
- Solvent fluid suitable for cleaning, such as iso-propyl alcohol (IPA).
- Fine lubricating oil formulated for use on plastic models.
- Fine 'low shear' lubricating grease.
- Rolling road saddles and suitable track or a rolling road unit.
- A power pack that delivers a controlled 12v DC supply.
- Leads with crocodile clips for easy connection to track.

LUBRICANTS AND CLEANERS

During the running-in process, the mechanism will bed gears and bearings into place. The lubricant applied to them at the factory when the model was first assembled is an important factor in this process. No matter how fine the mechanism is straight from the box, lubricant may dry out in transit and may need to be reapplied before the model is operated. Some manufacturers suggest that light lubrication is needed before a model is operated for the first time.

This is one reason why instruction leaflets should always be read first in order to see if there is any warranty requirement for lubrication before operation.

There are several choices of lubricant suitable for plastic models with paint finishes. Take care to select only those that are 'plastic safe' and stick with brands such as Carr's and Hob-e-Lube, which are specially formulated for use in plastic models. Carr's offers a fine lubricating oil based on silicone technology, which is designed to be of low viscosity but will not creep into places it is not wanted. The same brand includes a silicone grease that has a low shear strength for minimum resistance and high retention, which prevents it from flying off gears and other rotating components. It is formulated for gears with a sliding action, such as worm gears, and those that are not enclosed. Both lubricants are suitable for treating model locomotive mechanisms produced by today's mainstream manufacturers.

The Hob-e-Lube range, although more commonly used in North America, is also available in the UK. The range is ideal for painted plastic models which it will not degrade. Like all lubricants, it is designed to work with close tolerance mechanisms with low friction, high retention and low creep characteristics. Of the range of seven lubricants, the 'Ultra-Lite' oil is suitable for very close tolerance applications such as locomotive valve gear, while the 'Lite' oil is developed for medium-duty applications such as axles and bearings. Gear lube is offered for use on gears, whilst the 'Moly' grease is formulated for gears, axles and other high-friction applications. (For further information on the use of lubrication in routine maintenance, see Chapter 7.)

FIRST INSPECTION

As exciting as buying a new model can be, you should resist the temptation to plonk it straight on your layout and run it as you would any other model in your collection. There are several good reasons for this and, as I have discovered from experience, a new model may have a hidden defect that manifests itself when run on the layout straight from the box.

That exciting moment we all enjoy in the hobby has come around once again: the acquisition of a new model for the layout.

Here's why the instruction leaflet is so important: it is very easy to forget about packing and transit brackets that will hinder your attempt to run the model for the first time. Next stop: the workbench!

A crosshead jewellers' screwdriver makes short work of loosening the screws that hold the brackets in place. Reading the instructions at this point is important because in this model the screws must be refitted and tightened up again.

Many new models now come complete with a small bag of details for the purchaser to fit. The Hornby Standard Class 4 (4MT) model shown here remains to be fitted with a variety of details including brake rigging. Leave the details alone until the model has been checked and run-in.

Another Hornby steam locomotive model made to contemporary standards is this delightful Southern Railway T9 4-4-0 locomotive. Note the comprehensive instruction leaflet and transit bracket. Both should be retained in the box after the model has been introduced to the layout.

Removing the transit bracket from the Hornby T9. Many Hornby locomotives are so fitted, including its Class 43 High Speed Train power car model.

As many wheels as possible are fitted with current collection pickups, including those on the tender of steam locomotives. An electrical jumper cable and mini plug and socket arrangement are often used to connect the tender and locomotive, electrically speaking.

The Hornby T9 also comes with a variety of detailing parts, hence its rather minimalist appearance in this picture. Information on the fitting of add-on parts and nameplates will be found in Chapter 2.

A rolling road is an invaluable device for the static testing of models. This can take the form of a loco testing and running-in station or simple but precision roller units that fit to model railway track, such as these Bachrus rolling road 'saddles'. Some of the Bachrus range can be adjusted for different gauges and some are designed to work with a scale speed reader intended for models fitted with a speed matching decoder.

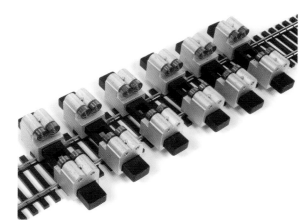

A locomotive undergoes static testing on Bachrus 'saddles'. Each wheel set sits on a single saddle, which is fitted with tiny rollers that rotate under the locomotive wheels. They also conduct electricity from the track to the wheels. A model can be properly run-in on such a static testing device.

Bachmann produces a very competent model of the English Electric Class 37 and has released various versions of it in different liveries. This model of 37 428 'David Lloyd George' is equipped with 6-axle drive, a five-pole motor, twin flywheels, a decent block of weight in the form of a die-cast chassis frame and RP25 profile wheels. It was taking a turn on Bachrus rolling road saddles before being placed in traffic.

It could be as simple as a misaligned coupling, a minor fault that could cause irreparable damage to a turnout should it catch on a running rail. Or perhaps something out of alignment inside the bodyshell may work loose on the first run, binding the mechanism and causing the motor to burn out before you can reach the model or turn the power off.

A workbench inspection of the new model before subjecting the model to a couple of hours of running in a controlled environment may detect any problems early on and save a great deal of trouble. Running-in time is also used to good effect to break a model in gently by bedding in the bearings and distributing lubricant, and to see if there are any defects that may result in the need to return the model to the manufacturer for a warranty repair. After all, locomotive models can take a pretty big bite out

of the modelling budget and the higher the price tag, the greater the expectation from performance. Consequently, spending some time on 'commissioning' a locomotive before placing it in service will deliver benefits in terms of better running and a reduction in wear and tear over time as the lubrication applied at the factory is worked into all moving parts and dirt is removed.

I have a fairly simple regime for the introduction of new models to my collection, to prepare them for fleet service on my layout and to ensure that defects are found before the model is subject to any detailing, conversion to Digital Command Control (DCC) and fitting of scale wheels. If your new model is not running well, there is little point in changing the wheels, fitting a DCC decoder or detailing it: that won't improve performance! Most certainly, a

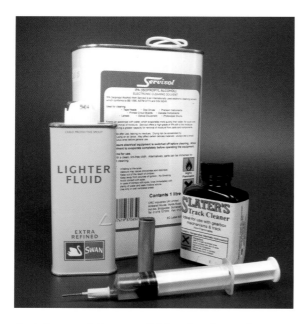

Certain materials are useful for cleaning and preparation including wheel and mechanism cleaner, isopropyl alcohol (also known as rubbing alcohol) suitable for cleaning excess oil and grease from wheels, current collection pickups and gears, together with model oil and grease for re-lubrication.

decoder will not much improve a steam locomotive if the valve gear is bent and causing a knock in the chassis. You may think that testing should have been done at the model shop where the original purchase was made. Many models, however, are purchased by mail order and it is not safe to assume that the retailer will have tested the model before dispatch unless you know the retailer extremely well. Even if you know that the model has been tested at the shop, it is nonetheless advisable to make a thorough check and run it in when you get it home.

The first stage after removing the model from the box is to read the service leaflet before giving the model a thorough visual inspection to detect any loose parts or components that may affect its performance or could cause damage if they fell off during operation. Sometimes it may be necessary to

return the model to the shop should you discover damaged detailing parts or that something is visually wrong with the mechanism. Bogie side frames and baseplates are removed so that the gears may be checked to see if there is any fluff, dirt or particles of metal that may cause wear and indifferent running. Also check that there is sufficient lubrication before you run the model. The model should be placed in a suitable cradle to protect it when inspecting the running gear and underframe.

The visual inspection continues by checking the wheels to see that they comply with accepted standards for gauge and back-to-back measurements, because some of my models are not converted to a closer-to-scale gauge so they can be operated on club layouts. This examination is undertaken with a back-to-back gauge and adjustments are made if necessary.

Once satisfied that the model is correctly gauged, power is applied to the model via leads from a simple analogue controller. This enables me to check that the wheels are concentric and that no alarming squeals, grinding or grating noises are coming from the mechanism. Such symptoms should be investigated and if they cannot be eliminated the model should be returned for repair.

In all fairness, I have found very few faults during this first inspection with locomotives I have bought over the years. However, my inspection regime has picked up the odd problem that could have developed into a frustrating and expensive issue later on. Examples of faults I have discovered on new models include:

- Misaligned couplings on a variety of models: simple to repair but could damage track if they are allowed to droop.
- A Hornby Class 60 with a front buffer beam fairing detached and likely to foul lineside details.
- A Bachmann Class 08 shunter with a broken coupling rod.
- Pickups that do not touch the back of the wheels in several cases. No juice collected from the track means no go!

- Current pickups out of alignment to the extent they foul spokes on the driving wheels of steam locomotives, with binding of the chassis the inevitable result.
- Obviously loose wires: simple to fix but can mean a model either does not run or the wires touch a flywheel or become tangled with a drive shaft.
- Excessive lubrication that becomes apparent when the model is run for the first time. This is better cleaned away before moving parts throw it all over the interior of the bodyshell.
- Missing screws.
- Misaligned wheels that cause binding and wobbly motion.

WHY INSTRUCTION LEAFLETS ARE IMPORTANT

Read and retain instruction leaflets provided by the manufacturers. They often show exploded diagrams of models, the catalogue numbers for spare parts and indicate lubrication points. The screw locations will be marked in place together with advice on how to remove the bodyshell without damaging fine detail. In short, they are the mini-service manual for that particular model and may provide advice for what may be a unique model. At the very least, when installing a decoder for DCC operation, the instructions will tell you what type of DCC interface socket is inside and where to find the body retaining screws and clips.

It is unfortunate that some models may arrive with excessive amounts of lubrication in the mechanism. One of the first checks is to look for problems like this where too much grease has been applied.

Another situation where grease has been liberally applied to everything, ending up on the back of wheels and on the current collection pickups. Clearly, electrical conductivity will be seriously impaired unless the grease is cleaned away and the pickups readjusted; here they did not meet the back of the wheel either.

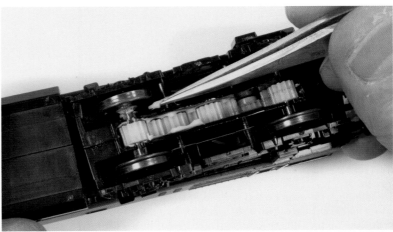

DCC onboard and digital sound locomotives will be furnished with an additional instruction sheet giving details of the installed decoder, its operation, functions and Configuration Variables setting (CVs). This too should be kept in the box or in a safe place for further reference. In short: don't throw leaflets away!

WHAT'S UNDER THE BODYSHELL

Nervous about what you might find under the bonnet? Reluctant to take a peek at how your prized engine actually functions? You should become familiar with the workings of your models so they can be properly maintained and cleaned in order to keep the layout running smoothly. Fortunately, the days of pancake 'ringfield' motors and weedy drives not even capable of pulling a feather off a table are long gone, although some modellers may still have a few models equipped with such old motors left in their collections. I am no exception, having retained a number of Lima Class 73s since no improved model

of this locomotive has been produced at the time of writing.

In their place, modellers are now enjoying the benefits of skew wound five-pole motors, sophisticated electronics including DCC interface sockets and sound decoders, together with a decent amount of ballast weight to optimize haulage performance. Steam locomotive collectors are seeing the end of tender drives and ringfield type motors in favour of locomotive-fitted drives connected to all of the driving wheels. Internal improvements have, fortunately, matched the considerable improvement in external and cosmetic detail, and certainly nowhere more so than in models of modern prototypes.

There is a great deal of sophistication tucked away within the bodyshell of a diesel electric locomotive model, just as in the mechanism and electronics of full-size diesel and electric locomotives. The mechanism found in new-generation models from all of the mainstream manufacturers, including Hornby, Heljan, Bachmann, Dapol and ViTrains, is very sophisticated. When first taking a bodyshell off a

Something is the cause of an intense discussion between these volunteers on the Great Central Railway as diesel electric shunter No. 3101 sits with its engine compartment doors and roof panel open. What is actually under the bonnet of our model locomotives is also worthy of a closer look.

A typical model of a diesel electric locomotive featuring a heavy die-cast chassis block and no visible moving parts. This is a Bachmann Class 45, introduced in 2009, with 6-axle drive, DCC interface socket, working running lights and a powerful, twin flywheel drive mechanism with a low maintenance requirement – but not a lot of the mechanism can be seen!

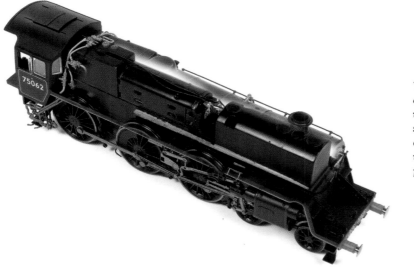

The once common practice of fitting a ringfield motor to the tender of a OO gauge steam locomotive is no longer acceptable practice: the motor, together with its drive train, is fitted to the locomotive itself.

The Hornby T9 reveals its inner workings including a five-pole motor and worm gear train driving all of the axles of the driving wheels via the coupling rods.

model, a newcomer to the hobby may be amazed at what they find, even if the service sheet offers a hint as to what is inside. The motor is usually mounted in the middle of a large die-cast chassis frame that contributes to the model's weight. A flywheel will be attached to one or both motor shafts, storing kinetic energy that translates to inertia when a locomotive hits a dead spot on the track, carrying it as if it has momentum like a full-size locomotive: this is a simple addition to the mechanism that improves the driving experience. Flexible couplings and drive shafts transmit power to the bogies via gear towers designed with the correct ratio of spur gears to divide the movement energy over all of the axles in the bogie. It is worth noting that not all axles in a three-axle bogie are powered on some models, including Heljan Class 47s and ViTrains Class 37s and Class 47s.

The result is a smooth-running locomotive with inertia and a feeling of momentum that adds to the driving experience. By having most, if not all, axles driven (the axles of each wheel set being bushed in a proper brass or phosphor bronze bearing for durability) the necessary tractive effort is provided to pull decent length trains. Electrical reliability comes as a result of the greater mass of modern-built locomotive models and the provision of electrical pickups on all wheels; even bogie wheels of steam locomotives will be fitted with pickups in some cases. All of this technical innovation helps to keep trains running without hesitation and lights flicker-free during operation.

For those dipping their toes in the world of Digital Command Control, manufacturers of OO gauge models now routinely equip the internal circuits of most models (when space permits) with an 8-pin DCC socket (to American NMRA and European MOROP NEM standards) for the simple installation of a decoder. Bachmann has introduced a 21-pin socket for which adapters are available. As a point of interest, the 6-pin interface socket has become standard for N gauge, again set out in NMRA and MOROP NEM specifications, and is also being adopted for some OO gauge models where space is too tight for a decoder designed for use with 8-pin

sockets. Examples include the 2010 release of the Bachmann Class 03 shunter.

The following sequence of photographs labels the common components of models from several manufacturers of British outline OO gauge equipment that are typical of what you should expect to find today. It is to be hoped that they will help with identification of parts for maintenance purposes or when converting models to DCC. Some are now supplied with a DCC decoder, making that process easier for the inexperienced modeller. Remember, when viewing these images, that there may be some variation between production runs of a model as improvements to the design are applied.

LIMA CLASS 117 DMU AND CLASS 73

Two models likely to be found in many modellers' collections are the Lima Class 117 DMU, a popular model for a variety of reasons (and yet to be re-released by Hornby since its acquisition of the Lima brand), together with the Class 73. The Class 117 model was equipped with a three-pole ringfield motor of varying levels of performance, but crude and difficult to control without the benefit of a flywheel to smooth out performance. However, it responds well to very good quality decoders and equally to careful fine tuning and running-in if the drive is basically sound. Not all of them were worth a second of workbench time, but in recent years an upgrade conversion for this basic type of ringfield motor has become available (see Chapter 5).

The basic mechanism in this model is simple: no circuit board, no lighting and a simple wire connection from the unpowered bogie, where current is collected from one side only. The power bogie itself has a direct connection between the carbon brush retainer and the wheel pickups that collects current from one side only, the opposite side to that on the unpowered bogie. The result is unreliability due to inadequate power supply, something that is simple to remedy by adding more pickups and wiring.

The Lima Class 73 (and other models in Lima's British outline range) have a similar arrangement to the Class 117, although some variation in the 'ring-

Despite the popularity of the former Lima Class 117 DMU among both modern and transition era modellers, Hornby has yet to re-release it with a new power bogie. It may be acquired second-hand, however, usually with the old ringfield motor drive that invariably needs much tender loving care to prod it into some sort of performance.

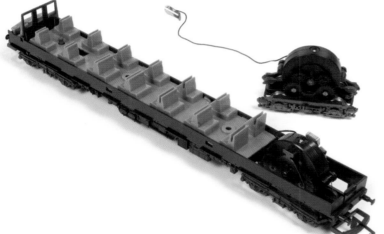

The crude nature of former Lima models is cruelly exposed when the body is removed. As can be seen, the pancake style ringfield motor is pretty rough and is the Achilles heel of this genre of models. The one in the top right of the picture is slightly different in design but has the same running characteristics and the same faults.

The typical arrangement in Lima models, the only variation between them being the number of axles in each bogie. A large lump of metal forms a crude ballast weight, while a single wire connects the unpowered bogie to the motor. (A) Motor casing; (B) ballast weight; (C) single pickup connection to the unpowered bogie; (D) exposed wire connection to power bogie pickups; (E) carbon brush and spring holder.

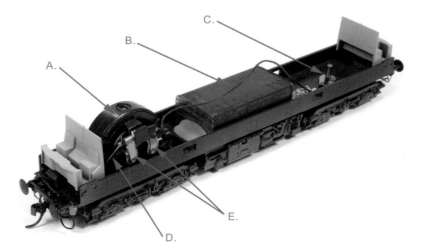

Very specific maintenance is required to ensure that the motor spindle does not become too dry and carbon brushes are not allowed to become too worn so that the internal retaining springs rub against the commutator.

field' motor can be observed. Despite the relatively high cost of these models when on general release, the drives are crude and often unworkable. That said, if you did get a good one it was worth refining and fine tuning, because they could be beaten into submission. All sorts of ideas, some of which are now the stuff of legend, floated around about how to refine these beasts, including the use of tooth-paste as a lubricant to get the noisy gear trains to settle down. In reality, the handful left in service in my collection run smoothly due more to their high mileage, careful maintenance and use of a suitable lubricant than to anything else. 'Moly' grease lubri-cant or Carr's micro grease product is ideal for gears with a high level of sliding contact as found on this type of mechanism.

UPGRADED FORMER LIMA CLASS 73 BY HORNBY

Hornby was quick to recognize the popularity of the former Lima Class 73 (former Southern Region electro diesel locomotive) and set to work to upgrade the underframe and replace the ringfield motor with one using a five-pole skew wound motor. The bogies were updated with NEM coupling pockets, the pickups were improved and an 8-pin NEM decoder socket included. The result is a better performing model with smoother control. However, you have to choose your decoders carefully to achieve the best performance and the model relies on traction tyres for grip. In reality, the new power bogie is a

poor relation to the high technology drives being applied to other Hornby models such as those fea-tured in this chapter and leaves the door open for the model to be further upgraded.

The format is common to all of the former Lima models re-released by Hornby: a new single power bogie and upgrading of bogies and couplings. The format has been applied to the Class 37, 55, 59 and 66 together with the Class 121 single-car DMU and Class 156 Sprinter. The same basic power bogie was also applied to the 2009 release of the Class 153 single-car Sprinter unit.

BACHMANN CLASS 20 (2009 RELEASE)

Bachmann has been steadily upgrading its Class 20 and the model featured in this chapter is a good example of a refined all-wheel-drive, four-axle diesel loco chassis with centrally fitted five-pole motor, twin flywheels and drive shafts with flexible cou-plings. The result is a smooth-running chassis with very refined slow speed control. Whilst no lighting circuits are fitted to this model, it is equipped with a 21-pin DCC interface socket (the earlier releases had an 8-pin socket) and features pickups on all wheels for good current collection. A digital sound and DCC onboard version is also available.

The format of this underframe and mechanism is also featured in Bachmann's Class 24 and 25, although with a wider die-cast chassis frame, result-ing in equally refined operation.

Hornby re-released the former Lima Class 73 in various liveries during 2008. Two examples are shown in this picture, both of which have had some retooling done to equip them with a new drive bogie, DCC interface socket and NEM coupling pockets.

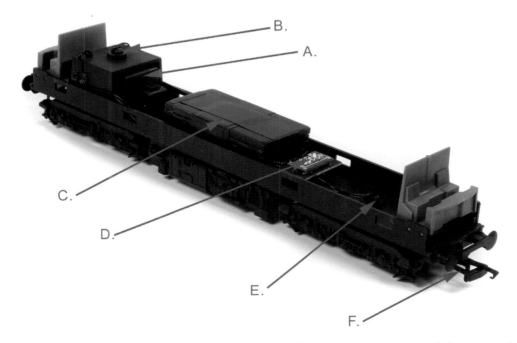

The new chassis for the Class 73 is typical of the re-released Lima range with an upgraded motor and slightly less crude ballast weight. (A) A single motor bogie with a five-pole skew wound motor; (B) a simple clip forms the bogie pivot; (C) ballast weight; (D) DCC interface socket; (E) unpowered bogie pivot; (F) tension lock couplings fitted to NEM coupling pockets.

Bachmann has produced several versions of its Class 20 model, of which one of the latest features train reporting head code boxes with 'domino' marker dots.

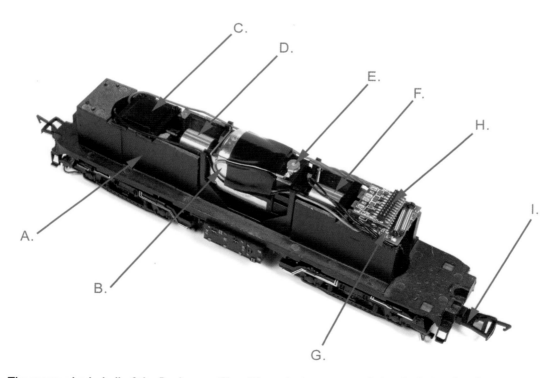

The narrow bodyshell of the Bachmann Class 20 results in an unusual chassis design that features a frame-mounted motor, Cardan shafts and all-wheel drive, which is quite different to the arrangement in the former Lima Class 73 (see above). (A) Large die-cast metal chassis frame; (B) five-pole motor fitted to the chassis frame; (C) gear tower cover, with gears concealed by the chassis frame; (D) brass flywheel; (E) motor terminals located on top and underneath; (F) second flywheel; (G) electronics circuit board; (H) 21-pin DCC interface connector with dummy plug fitted; (I) NEM coupling pockets fitted to the bogies.

BACHMANN (MID-LIFE)
CLASS 47 (2009 RELEASE)

Based on the Class 57 chassis, the Bachmann OO gauge Class 47 has been released in two batches, both with the same basic chassis arrangements of a six-axle drive powered by a five-pole can motor mounted in a die-cast frame. It features twin fly-wheels and drive shafts connected to bogie gear towers for all-wheel drive. It is a powerful chassis that, when combined with a weight nearing 500g, can pull trains of an impressive length. No traction tyres are fitted: none are needed.

The mid-life version of the Class 47 released by Bachmann in 2009 included this model of British Rail Parcels Sector Class 47 No. 47 474.

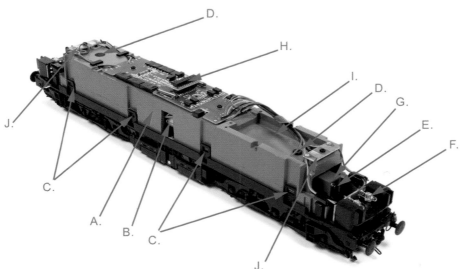

The Class 47 drive mechanism powers all six axles, making the model capable of hauling large trains. The carefully engineered die-cast chassis, resulting in an overall weight of almost half a kilo, has an impressive specification and is a contributing factor to the impressive haulage capacity of this model. (A) die-cast metal chassis frame; (B) five-pole skew wound motor; (C) the underframe moulding is clipped to the chassis frame; (D) bogies are fixed to the chassis using screws; (E) driveshaft ends are just visible; (F) lighting circuit board (both ends); (G) top of the bogie gear tower; (H) 21-pin DCC interface connector with dummy plug fitted; (I) recess in die-cast frame to accommodate digital sound speaker; (J) cab light contacts.

One minor problem identified in Bachmann six-axle drive models, including later releases of the Class 37, Class 57, 'Deltic' and Class 66, is that the centre axle rides slightly proud of the two outer axles of each bogie. The problem can be seen when the model is placed on a sheet of plate glass and the bogie rocked vertically about the middle axle. This prevents all of the wheels from making direct contact with the track and so reduces the effective tractive effort. While this presents few problems when such a model is used on standard OO gauge layouts with the RP25-110 wheels fitted to Bachmann models, it becomes an issue after re-wheeling with finescale wheels, such as RP25-88 profile wheels, or those used by Scalefour modellers. Derailments become more common as the leading axle no longer guides the locomotive into curves as the bogie sits down on the rear axle when power is applied, and there is less flange to accommodate the 0.5mm or so of lift. The slightest irregularity of the track soon brings the locomotive off and into the ballast.

The cure is straightforward: shave a small amount of plastic (about 0.5mm) from the inside of the bogie frame mount that holds the brass axle bushes of the middle axle. This allows the middle axle to sit into the frame a little further without disrupting the mesh of the gears, which fortunately is quite loose.

VITRAINS CLASS 47

The six-axle chassis used by ViTrains in both its Class 37 and Class 47 is an interesting development. There is a large five-pole motor fitted to a die-cast chassis frame driving the wheels of both bogies via drive shafts, flywheels and gear towers. The design is a four-axle drive with unpowered middle axles in each bogie, which are loose and unsprung. Current collection is via the outer axles of each bogie, where stiff wires run in a groove on the back of each wheel rather than making contact with the rear face using sprung phosphor bronze pickups more commonly found on Bachmann and Hornby models.

The four-axle drive is as powerful as most other models of this genre and the loose middle axle means that the issue with Bachmann six-axle models (see above) is avoided, but with the loss of some tractive effort. The middle axle would benefit from some springing to improve road holding. The use of 2mm diameter axles makes the model straightforward to convert to EM and P4 gauge using 14mm diameter rolling stock wheels or an economy conversion pack from Ultrascale. However, the pickup arrangement would require some revision.

Hornby and Bachmann are not the only companies offering a OO gauge model of the Class 47. ViTrains produces an accurate model with a modern drive system. One feature is that the model has many standalone detailing parts that are not fitted to the model but left to the purchaser to fit, so explaining the very plain appearance of the locomotive shown here.

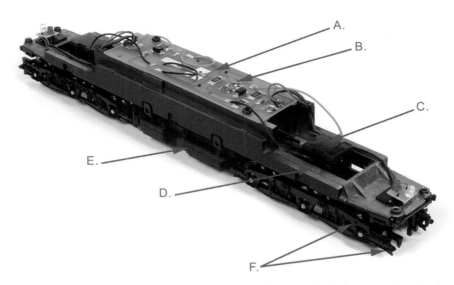

The underframe and drive follows a similar format to the Bachmann Class 47, except that the ViTrains model has only four driven axles out of the six with the central axle on both bogies left unpowered. (A) The circuit board is simple in design compared to Bachmann and Hornby models; (B) DCC interface socket with jumper clips for analogue operation; (C) bogie gear tower with worm drive at the top; (D) large die-cast chassis frame; (E) fuel tanks simply clip to the chassis frame making it easy to represent the different types used on Class 47s; (F) locating holes for fitting separately supplied standalone parts.

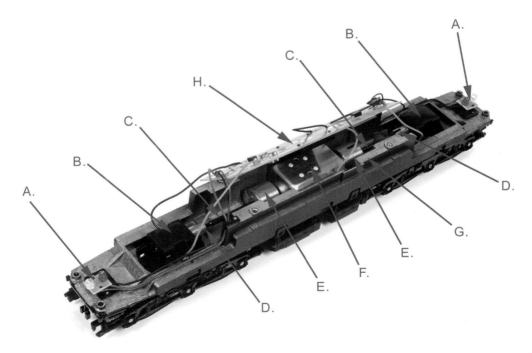

Much more detail of the ViTrains Class 47 drive mechanism can be seen when the circuit board is removed: (A) the model is fitted with working head and tail lights; (B) top of the bogie gear tower; (C) driveshaft with flexible couplings at each end; (D) flexible couplings; (E) twin brass flywheels; (F) five-pole motor; (G) die-cast chassis frame encloses the motor and holds it in place; (H) circuit board.

BACHMANN CLASS 45 (2009 RELEASE)

Another very powerful six-axle drive chassis using the same basic arrangement as used in the Bachmann Class 47 model, except for the unpowered load-bearing wheel in the front of each bogie. Notably, and in common with many Bachmann drives, the moving parts are concealed within a big and heavy die-cast chassis frame. Access to check the gear towers and other moving parts can be gained by simply unscrewing the bogies and dropping them out for inspection and lubrication. All of the driven wheels pick up current via phosphor bronze contacts on the rear face of each wheel and power is distributed to the motor and lighting circuits via a large circuit board located on top of the chassis. A 21-pin decoder socket is included in the design.

The Bachmann Class 45 'Peak' locomotive features a powerful all-wheel-drive mechanism, excluding the small pony truck wheels at the front of each bogie. This is a powerful and heavy model that runs well and reliably thanks to twin brass flywheels, all-wheel pickup for current and around half a kilo of weight.

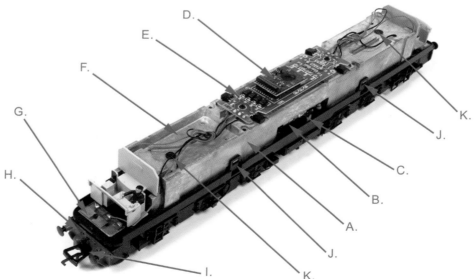

Internally, the story is beginning to look familiar with these new-generation models. The motor is large and has five poles. The die-cast chassis is specially engineered for the model and there is room for both digital decoder and digital sound speaker. Working lights and illuminated head codes come as standard. (A) Specially engineered die-cast frame; (B) five-pole skew wound motor; (C) TV interference suppression capacitor; (D) 21-pin digital decoder (factory fitted in the case of this particular model); (E) electronic circuit board distributing power to running lights and motor; (F) space provided in the die-cast frame for a digital sound speaker; (G) contacts for running lights and head code illumination; (H) holes provided in the buffer beams for the fitting of supplied standalone parts; (I) NEM coupling pockets are fitted to the bogies.

HORNBY CLASS 60

At 660g in weight, the Hornby Class 60 is a bit of a monster capable of towing a sizeable train, just like the full-size locomotives. It is a model of a very big freight engine with high tractive effort that is at home on oil trains, block steel and aggregate traffic. The motor is built into a die-cast chassis frame with the now familiar drive shafts, flexible couplings and all-wheel-drive in each bogie. The model has very flexible bogie frames and the wheels all make contact with the track, ensuring that the full tractive effort is applied. Notable is the space available for a decoder and the circuit board supplying lighting circuits via contacts under each cab. The choice of decoder can be tricky: this is a case of horses for courses because the five-pole motor likes certain characteristics and some BEMF decoders do not suit it at all well.

Hornby offers a very impressive model of the Class 60 heavy freight engine built for BR Railfreight in the early 1990s. Its sophisticated mechanism and mass of more than 600g ensures the model can perform as well as the full-size locomotives – scaled down, of course!

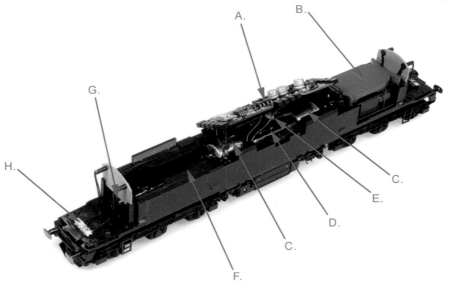

Technical specifications of the Hornby Class 60: (A) circuit board for lighting and power to the motor (shown loose from the chassis frame); (B) some models such as the Class 60 are equipped with internal detailing that can be seen through etched grilles in the bodyshell; (C) two brass flywheels are fitted to the motor shaft on either side of the motor; (D) five-pole skew wound motor; (E) TV interference suppression (EMC) capacitor; (F) Cardan or drive shaft together with coupling to the bogie gear tower; (G) wiring for the lighting circuits is routed over the cab bulkheads to keep the wires clear of the mechanism; (H) Electrical contacts for lighting circuits fitted to the bodyshell.

BACHMANN 'PANNIER TANK' LOCOMOTIVE

The simplest arrangement in a steam locomotive is demonstrated by the Bachmann 'pannier tank' locomotive. The chassis is die-cast with wheels retained from the underside by a keeper plate screwed in place. The motor is a simple can with a worm gear attached to the single rotor shaft. This drives a single gear tower to the rear axle, where the wheels are all driven via the coupling rods. The DCC decoder is a factory-installed DCC onboard model with the decoder connected to an 8-pin DCC interface socket. No lights are fitted to this model and traction tyres are not used either.

Small tank engines are very appealing and generally have quite simple mechanisms. The challenge for the manufacturer today is to provide sufficient weight within the model for good haulage capacity but allow sufficient room for a digital decoder in what is usually a narrow boiler and smoke box. Just to make life a little more interesting for the manufacturer, modellers are increasingly demanding detailed cab interiors, which means the motor has to be placed sufficiently forward on the locomotive chassis to keep the cab clear of obstructions.

Internally this Bachmann locomotive has a very simple arrangement and was supplied from the factory with the decoder already installed to an 8-pin DCC interface socket (F). A small five-pole motor (A) drives a single worm gear (B), which transmits power via spur gears (C) to one driven axle. Motion is transmitted to all of the wheels using the coupling rods. There is a direct wired connection to each motor terminal (D) from the small circuit board (E).

HORNBY CLASS 08/09 DIESEL ELECTRIC SHUNTING LOCOMOTIVE

Both Hornby and Bachmann offer a Class 08/09 diesel electric shunting locomotive with very similar chassis construction. This type of locomotive is made more complex by having outside frames and cranks together with coupling rods. This is clearly a challenging locomotive to build economically, so to have two smooth-running and powerful off-the-shelf models of it is remarkable. The Hornby model is featured, with a DCC interface socket and a five-pole motor driving one axle via a gear tower. All wheels are powered, the motion being transferred by the coupling rods, which makes maintaining the quartering of the wheels very important, as it is in a steam locomotive. The extended axles have squared ends that match square mounting holes in the cranks. This prevents the cranks slipping on the axles, but they are prone to damage, so tough handling is definitely not a good idea. For more on the model's structure, see a re-wheeling project in Chapter 3 and the repair of a damaged model in Chapter 7.

The Hornby Class 08/09 shunter has impressive haulage capability to match its good looks and that is thanks to the large amount of die-cast metal within the bodyshell. While there is room for a decoder, anything more may need the removal of one of the weights that are screwed in place.

The highly acclaimed Hornby Class 08/09 shunter, a prominent part of the company's range, is seen at work on the author's layout.

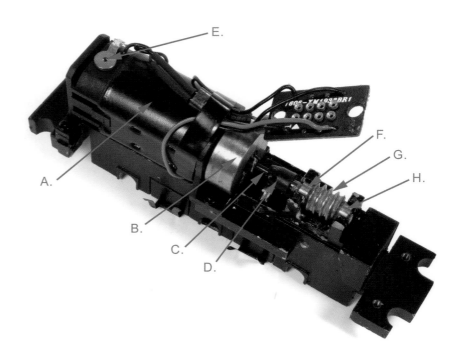

Details of the Hornby Class 08/09 drive mechanism shown after the removal of the separate die-cast weight from the chassis: (A) five-pole motor; (B) single flywheel; (C) short drive shaft; (D) flexible coupling; (E) motor terminal; (F) worm gear shaft bearing [one at each end of the worm gear (H)]; (G) worm gear.

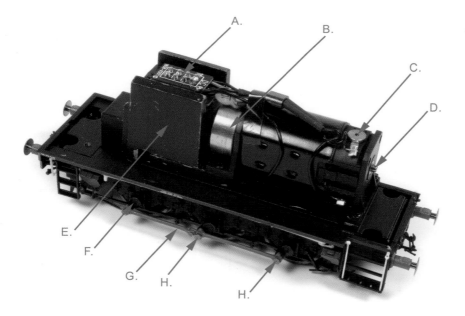

The same challenge exists with the Class 08/09 shunter as with other small locomotives of this type, including the Bachmann tank engine featured above: ensuring enough weight for traction but leaving sufficient room for a decoder. (A) 8-pin DCC interface socket; (B) single flywheel; (C) motor terminals are located on both top and bottom of the motor; (D) end of motor rotor shaft; (E) a separately fitted chassis weight encloses the single gear tower; (F) outside cranks; (G) coupling rods; (H) coupling rod securing pins.

HORNBY SOUTHERN RAILWAY T9

A delightful model with a competent chassis featuring the drive motor in the locomotive together with enough die-cast metal to provide good haulage characteristics. The model is assisted with traction tyres on both wheels of the driven axle, which is powered via a single gear tower. The second driven axle is powered via the coupling rods. The motor is positioned forward to leave the cab clear for some exquisite detailing, yet is large enough to provide power to the driving wheels. This type of locomotive is always going to be challenging for Hornby to build with good haulage characteristics (the M7 is in a similar situation) because the inherently lightweight nature of the model makes applying power to the rails tricky, hence the use of traction tyres.

The tender houses electrical pickups and a sub-miniature plug and socket arrangement so that current can be transmitted to the motor. The 8-pin DCC socket is also located in the tender, where there is more than enough room to accommodate a typical HO/OO gauge 1amp decoder and associated harness wires, or one of the direct plug and play decoders.

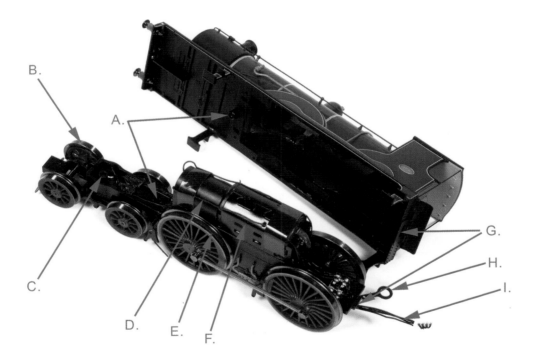

Another small locomotive with the motor and drive mechanism installed in the locomotive itself and not, as used to be common practice, in the tender. Since the locomotive is not particularly heavy, traction is improved by fitting rubber traction tyres to the powered axle. The second axle is also driven, but not directly, only through the coupling rods. (A) Body securing screw fixing point; (B) front bogie wheels are fitted with electrical pickups; (C) front bogie pivot; (D) gearbox and tower; (E) traction tyres fitted to the directly driven wheels; (F) small, but powerful, five-pole motor; (G) rear body fixing clip; (H) tender coupling; (I) electrical jumper cables connect tender to the locomotive.

Underside of the Hornby T9 steam locomotive with the wheel keeper plate removed, revealing the final drive gear and phosphor bronze wiper pickups.

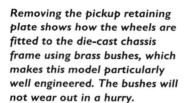

Removing the pickup retaining plate shows how the wheels are fitted to the die-cast chassis frame using brass bushes, which makes this model particularly well engineered. The bushes will not wear out in a hurry.

Some electrical equipment, including an 8-pin DCC interface socket (A), is located logically in the tender of the Hornby T9 steam locomotive, where there is plenty of room for a typical OO/HO gauge 1 Amp decoder. Other features include the TV interference suppression capacitor (C) and additional electrical pickups (B).

HORNBY BR STANDARD CLASS 4 (4MT)

This is a classic 4-6-0 locomotive design but modernized to the highest specification now available in the Hornby range. Gone are the old tender drives in favour of a powerful five-pole motor in the engine itself, delivering smooth performance to all three driving wheel axles via a single gear tower and the coupling rods.

There are no traction tyres fitted to this model because its tractive effort is more than adequate to haul a reasonably long train on the level. The tender has enough clear space for an 8-pin DCC interface socket and to accommodate a decoder. A subminiature plug and socket arrangement provides an electrical connection from the tender to the engine, while there is also a metal bar coupling for a mechanical connection.

Hornby's OO gauge BR Standard Class 4 is a new-generation model with an impressive specification and very fine running qualities. Care is needed to protect the delicate standalone detailing parts added to this model.

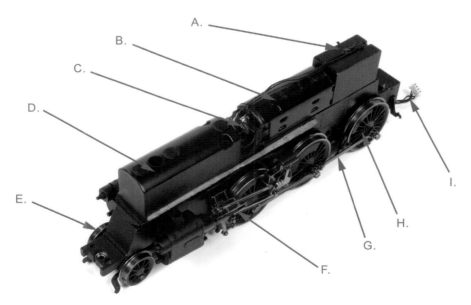

There is a great deal of ballast weight in the BR Standard Class 4, adding up to good haulage capacity. The DCC interface socket and additional current collection pickups are located in the tender. (A) Gear box and tower located to the rear of the engine; (B) long narrow motor; (C) the end of the motor shaft is just visible and accessible for any lubrication; (D) the additional ballast weight might make it difficult to fit a smoke unit; (E) bogie wheels are fitted with current pickups; (F) complex valve gear needs care to avoid binding of the mechanism; (G) coupling rods transmit motion to all driving wheels; (H) directly driven axle; (I) electrical jumper wires and plug for connection to the tender.

RUNNING-IN

With the visual inspection completed, running-in can commence. I prefer to use a rolling road for static running and testing so I can observe the model carefully on the workbench. Both eyes and ears are important to this process as they both detect important aspects of performance. Your nose may also come into play if there is the chance of electrical components becoming too warm if the model is labouring and drawing too much current. It is easier to detect slight knocks in the chassis of a steam locomotive or a misaligned wheel on a diesel when the model can be observed running from close quarters. Your hearing will tell you if a pickup is clicking against something or if the model is settling in as the sound of the mechanism changes and becomes smoother.

My preferred choice for static running tests is the Bachrus 50-series rolling road (six separate saddles designed to sit on ready-to-lay track) for 4mm scale models in OO and EM gauge because the 50-series saddles can be adjusted to suit various gauges and track from HO through to P4 gauge. The Bachrus rolling road saddle system has proven itself to be reliable in operation with analogue and DCC control on my workbench, being used with North American outline stock as well as my British outline models.

The saddles are placed on the track at the correct distance apart for the locomotive's wheelbase and the model is placed on the saddles, carefully checking that each wheel sits neatly between each pair of rollers. Once secure, it is run at half speed for between 15 and 30 minutes in either direction using a DC power pack and while under supervision. If there are no obvious signs of distress, the model is operated for a further 15 minutes in either direction at near full power. Usually all is well and defects are rarely found.

The model is returned to the inspection cradle and the bogie frames or chassis baseplates removed for further inspection. The level of lubrication is checked to see if it has worked into all moving parts and bearings: usually a squealing noise results from dry motor and shaft bearings, so listen for such an indication of poor lubrication levels. Remove the body and inspect the bogie gear towers and Cardan shafts too – they must be correctly lubricated for smooth operation and to reduce wear. Dirty grease and oil must be cleaned away because it retains dirt and particles of material that could cause premature wear in the future, an especially important point to remember with locos fitted with delrin plastic gear trains. Excess lubrication should be removed too and those areas that appear to lack lubrication should be gently oiled with a tiny drop of model mechanism oil applied on the end of a pin. Reassemble the model and subject it to a further 15-minute period of running, which can be extended if required. Some models take longer to settle down than others, but you will hear the change in the pace of the model for a given voltage as running-in progresses. In other words, the model speeds up and runs more quietly and with considerably less vibration.

Never be tempted to leave the model unattended when running on a rolling road, for should the mechanism bind, you must be present to take immediate action to prevent the motor from burning out or the mechanism from becoming damaged. My own testing track is located on a shelf next to my workbench, so test running can be undertaken when I am doing other modelling tasks and can supervise the process with both eyes and ears. Once the model is running smoothly, the body can be popped off and a decoder fitted. Testing of the decoder installation and allocating a unique address can all be done at the workbench before the model is placed on the layout for its first run. Persevere with running-in because it delivers significant benefits when the model is delivered to the layout for service.

TEST RUNNING ON THE LAYOUT

Usually a quick test is all that is needed to determine if the locomotive is ready for fleet service. A run up and down the layout, through junctions and past close lineside structures such as platforms, soon reveals if there are any problems. With that task completed, it's into service either as a pristine, out of the box model or until you find workbench time to add the detailing parts, make some further refinements, change the model's identity or apply some weathering (all aspects of modelling described in Chapter 5).

Test running, for me, is the opportunity to really refine the performance of a model and I will spend hours observing, listening, adjusting, tinkering and fiddling to improve slow speed control for shunting, the controllability of the model for smooth acceleration and deceleration and to prevent surging and hesitant running, all aspects of the model's performance that cannot be done on a rolling road.

As a new model circles around the layout, get down to track level and see how it runs through turnouts and crossings. Does it wobble or glide smoothly? Is there any interruption in power supply? Does it derail at certain locations or in random spots? Are the couplings catching the track in places? All of these are small problems simple to resolve, and solving them refines the operation of both layout and model. Occasionally a new model can reveal weaknesses in the layout and its track that were hitherto tolerated or not even noticed. Now is the time to resolve them before the next operating session. Have a small notebook to hand to record any problems that need attention. This is prototypical because the full-size railways document defects very carefully indeed. Call it a defect book if you like, and when working on models and the layout, refer to it to see what needs to be adjusted and repaired to keep things running well.

All of this effort pays off when your friends arrive for an operating session and the latest addition to the fleet performs beautifully, adding to the enjoyment of operating a model railway: poor performance spoils even the most beautifully detailed layout and can cause operators to become bored quite quickly. If a layout and its locomotives run well, getting your operators to return for another session is so much easier to do.

A pair of Lima Class 73s work along the mainline of the author's fixed layout (under construction when photographed) with a train of ballast hoppers. Careful maintenance means these veteran models can still earn their keep and remain in traffic since no new-generation model of the Class 73 is available at the time of writing.

Heljan Class 33s work a ballast train; the lead engine is new and is undergoing its first test run after workbench time to inspect and break it in. Performance with Heljan models is usually more than satisfactory straight from the box. When trial running is completed, the model will be detailed and weathered to match the one running behind it in digital 'consisting' mode.

Hornby Class 60s are generally regarded as among the company's finest diesel electric locomotive models. This one is also new and being run before being renumbered and detailed using the standalone parts supplied with it.

WHAT TO DO WHEN
SOMETHING GOES WRONG

Sometimes – and regrettably – a new model may have a fault that cannot be resolved through simple adjustment. Let's assume you have checked everything and done the correct running-in, yet still the model does not run smoothly, has intermittent power failure as indicated by the running lights flashing unacceptably, or it binds, squeals or makes other alarming noises. This is the time to contact the retailer to arrange for an exchange under warranty. You should have retained your original receipt and all the packaging if the model was purchased by mail order, together with the original box, sleeve, tissue paper and instruction leaflets, not to mention the transit brackets. Do not lose the packet of add-on details and handle the model particularly carefully, so as not to give the retailer any reason to refuse the return.

Fortunately, most model shops are run by modellers who understand the issues and they may have both the skills and spares to undertake a repair on the premises. Sometimes that is not possible, however, and the model has to be returned to the manufacturer for repair or exchange. You are within your rights to ask for a refund, and remember that the UK Distance Selling Regulations entitle you to a thirty-day no quibble return on mail ordered goods if you change your mind, even if it is not faulty. Do not expect to be refunded for postage charges, either those paid for the original order or any you need to pay to return the model. The model should be unused and returned with its original packaging and contents. Faulty models returned under warranty to a mail order business should either be exchanged for another or a refund offered, including all postage costs.

I am sure, while you have been reading this, that you have been wondering about the small packet of detailing parts included in the box with many new models. Those parts may include etched brass nameplates, air and vacuum brake pipes, brake linkages and, in the case of the ViTrains Class 47, a fairly large number of additional details that should be added to the model. The next chapter looks at the add-on parts, nameplates and options for fitting the more common types of couplings to NEM coupling boxes, including discussion of what the NEM coupling standard means and how their use affects the operation of your models.

CHAPTER TWO

FITTING FACTORY-SUPPLIED PARTS

Cast a casual glance over any locomotive, either steam or diesel electric, and you cannot fail to notice the small details: air and vacuum brake hoses, brackets and guards on the bogies, couplings, electrical jumper cables and a whole host of other things. It's increasingly common for model manufacturers to supply small details present on the full-size locomotives as standalone parts for the modeller to fit. All of those small details make the model and bring it closer to the prototype, as seen in this photograph of Southern Railway 4-6-0 No. 850 'Lord Nelson'. It enables the cost-effective production of models that can look as good as the prototype. But how are they applied?

INTRODUCTION

With a new model tested and running smoothly, attention usually turns to the sometimes large pile of finely moulded and etched detail parts left for the modeller to fit: parts that include almost anything from buffer beam fittings to nameplates, underframe parts to handrails, depending on the model and its manufacturer. Leaving it to the modeller to fix the finishing parts saves a great deal of money in not having to pay someone to do it at the factory, keeping the final cost to the modeller in check. For the newcomer to the hobby, however, that pile of detailing parts usually comes as a bit of a surprise: how are they applied to the model without making a mess of it?

It appears that some manufacturers assume that the purchaser of the locomotive, coach or wagon

has sufficient skill and knowledge to identify and secure the parts and nameplates without compromising what is likely to be an expensive model. Fortunately, there is usually an instruction leaflet that includes arrangement diagrams showing where each bit has to go. But, and it's a big one, few actually offer advice on glues or modelling tools, let alone the workbench techniques required to do a good job of add-on parts.

While on the subject of add-on parts and detailing packs, the workings of NEM coupling pockets can be something new too. How do they work and can they be better used? This chapter looks at the tools and materials required to complete the preparation of a new, contemporary standard model for the layout by showing how to attach all those pesky detailing parts, how to use NEM coupling pockets and how to apply nameplates without marring the paint finish.

Separate detailing parts can be as simple as handrails and brake pipes. The application technique requires tweezers, a steady hand and tiny amounts of adhesive.

Fitting all of the standalone parts is time consuming but will produce a very good looking model, as is the case with the Bachmann Deltic featured in this picture.

DETAILING PARTS

So, the little packet of plastic parts is open and sitting on the workbench. It's natural to expect that the parts will slip neatly into the holes moulded in the model without much more than gentle pressure. Well, many an experienced modeller has sworn and cussed over add-on parts supplied with an expensive model. They flick out of the tweezers holding them to become lost in the carpet. Since most are moulded from 'difficult plastics', which are usually hard and shiny, they are near impossible to glue with those adhesives usually found around the house, such as superglue. Anyway, in many cases those dratted holes are too small and have to be opened out with a small twist drill fitted to a pin

vice. You can also correctly guess that it is rare to be supplied with additional items: lose one and it's a call to the service centre to buy another add-on pack.

Despite these issues, it is a task that can be done by any modeller, new or experienced. With care, the right tools, good quality adhesives and careful reading of the instructions supplied with the model, it's an enjoyable part of adding a new model to the fleet. The end result will be a beautifully detailed model ready for traffic on the layout as the manufacturer intended, so the time spent at the workbench carefully fitting seemingly endless parts is well worth it.

There are some simple tools and materials you should have to hand, including tweezers capable of securely holding small parts, some clean cocktail sticks, a sharp modelling knife, cutting mat, a plastic lid from a Pringles tube (or something similar), fine-nose pliers, such as those used for jewellery making, and cyanoacrylate based superglue (CA glue) suitable for hard shiny plastics. Read the label on the glue bottle carefully before purchasing to ensure you buy the most appropriate type for the job.

Some tasks benefit from the use of a CA glue accelerator such as Zap Kicker, which is a liquid that freezes CA glue on contact: it saves a great deal of time. As usual with any time-saving material, there is a price to pay, and the modeller should be aware that such materials can cause CA glue to 'bloom', discolouring parts. If you are not prepared to touch up the paint work, avoid the use of accelerators. My personal favourite for gluing hard shiny plastics, often referred to as 'space age' plastics, is Poly Zap CA glue. Surprisingly low cost, it can bond pre-painted add-on parts without blooming. With the right surface preparation, this glue will bond those hard shiny plastics quite securely, too, when other adhesives will not touch them. Experiments with 'normal' household CA glue have been unsuccessful and solvent adhesives such as Plastic Weld will not have any effect at all with difficult plastics.

Before starting work, locate a piece of foam or similar to rest the model on the tabletop while working on it. Sometimes the foam insert from the model's box may be used. In some cases it is useful to partly dismantle the model before starting work: bogies can be unclipped, bodies removed to avoid damaging delicate parts and so on. With good light, adequate ventilation to chase the glue fumes away and a steady hand, you are ready to have a go. If you are still uncertain, practise with your materials and make a dry run assembly test without glue to be sure you are fitting things in the right place. A sharp scalpel can be used to remove parts from spares and trim away any moulding pips. Clean the parts in isopropyl alcohol (IPA) if you can to remove grease and moulding release fluid, so giving the glue a better chance of bonding securely.

The following models demonstrate the typical add-on detailing parts the modeller may encounter with a new model purchased today. Starting with the two Hornby steam locomotives detailed in the last chapter, I have also included the ViTrains Class 47, which is perhaps the most difficult of the diesel electric locomotives to complete ready for traffic. After following these projects, you should be well equipped to tackle anything that comes your way.

Steam locomotives typically come supplied with vacuum pipes, brake rigging, a spare coupling and a scale screw link coupling, as is the case with the Hornby T9. Some parts are not required for a working locomotive, but are only intended to add detail for showcases.

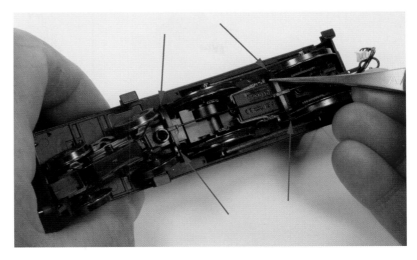

Brake rigging clips into the holes at the bottom of the brake shoes. Sometimes adhesive is needed to secure the rigging in place.

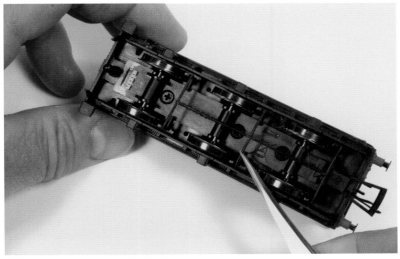

Tenders have brake rigging too. The same thing applies: the ends fit tiny holes in the base of each brake shoe.

Fitting a scale screw link coupling to the front of the Hornby T9 locomotive. If such detail is added to the front, it is not possible to use the supplied tension lock coupling or a different type designed to fit the NEM coupling pocket.

More detailing parts, this time for the Hornby 4MT model.

Brake rigging is not the only detail you may find lurking in the box. Other add-on details could include pipework to fit to the cylinders and other parts of the boiler. Some parts are not obvious to place, so read the instructions carefully to identify the locating holes.

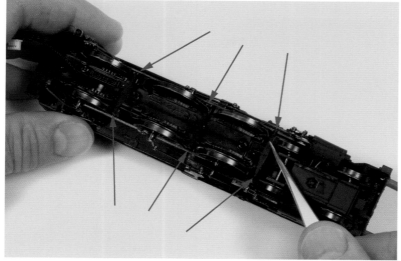

Brake rigging is shown being fitted to the Hornby 4MT locomotive. Don't forget to do the tender too and glue it so that it does not become loose when the model is in use. The results could be spectacular, if expensive.

VITRAINS CLASS 47

The ViTrains Class 47 holds the record for the greatest number of add-on parts supplied with a ready-to-run model – at the time of writing!

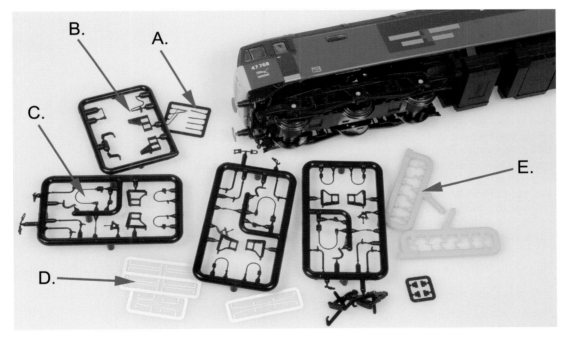

ABOVE: This looks more like a kit than a ready-to-run locomotive. Not all of these parts are applicable, so check them against the service sheet usually supplied with new models. The ViTrains Class 47 comes with etched metal windscreen wipers (A), bogie details (B), jumper cable detail (C) that is also shared with its Class 37 model (so not everything applies), metal handrails (D), couplings and lamp brackets (E).

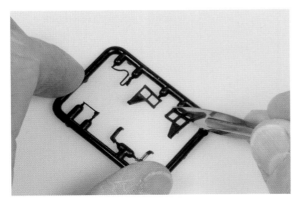

LEFT: A sharp scalpel is more than sufficient to remove the parts from the sprue. Use a special modellers' cutting mat to save the tabletop and extend the life of modelling knife blades.

Fine-nose tweezers are ideal for handling small parts such as the bogie footsteps illustrated here. Take care not to drop or ping parts into the carpet because there may not be a spare one on the sprue.

There will always be parts needing glue to secure them in place. Never apply glue to the model straight from the bottle. This is how so many models are irreparably damaged. Place a tiny amount in a plastic dish (top of a Pringles tube or a piece of plastic) and either dip the part in that to pick up a tiny spot of glue or use a cocktail stick to transfer it to the model. This picture shows a bogie guard being fitted to the Class 47 model.

Note the use of a piece of foam on which to rest the model while working on it. This will protect the paint finish and any details fitted to the opposite side.

BELOW: **Look for locating holes for all of the detailing parts. Occasionally a small diameter twist drill is needed to open up a hole so the part will fit.**

ABOVE: **Once the part is in place and the glue has grabbed, apply a tiny drop of superglue accelerator to freeze the glue. This speeds up the project and prevents stray glue from migrating to places you don't want it to when the model is turned over or handled. It's normal to have to hold the part in place when applying the accelerator solution if the glue does not immediately bond.**

Handrails are either plastic or metal on contemporary standard models. In this case, ViTrains supplies very neat metal handrails for its Class 47. They should be cut from the fret with a strong blade or snips.

Open up the handrail holes with either a drill bit of around 0.45mm diameter or with the sharp end of a pair of fine-nose tweezers – carefully. Don't overdo it because you need a tight fit to hold the handrails in place without using glue.

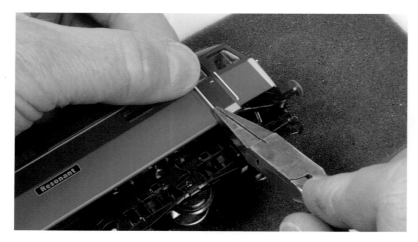

The handrails are carefully placed with fine-nose pliers and pressed into the holes, gently but firmly, one end at a time.

Using the same fine-nose pliers, firmly press the handrails in place. Avoid pushing them right up against the bodyshell surface. If you do this by accident, slip a blade between the body and handrail to adjust it.

The job should take only an hour or so to complete, even allowing for slow, careful work. This picture shows the sample ViTrains Class 47 fitted with roof aerials, windscreen wipers, jumper cables, speedometer cable, bogie fittings, foot steps, handrails and couplings. They make quite a difference to the appearance of a model and taking the time to do this task properly, with the correct adhesives, is well worthwhile.

NAMEPLATES AND PLAQUES

Named locomotives are quite common through railway history and diesel and electric era locomotives are no different. They are always attractive to modellers and one of the first improvements or detailing tasks that modellers attempt on their locomotives is to replace printed nameplates with etched ones. Etched plates, be they etched brass for steam locomotives or etched nickel silver and stainless steel for diesel and electric locomotives, do look considerably better because they usually have the relief that is lacking with printed detail. Things came to a head for diesel and electric modellers in the

1980s with the introduction of BR sector liveries, which not only included the traditional nameplate but depot plaques and cast double arrows too!

For the modeller who is keen to make this small improvement to what may already be a well-researched and well-applied livery, there are several manufacturers of etched nameplates and depot plaques for both modern era and steam era modelling. Fitting nameplates is one of those jobs that looks easy and can be easy on a good day at the modelling table. It is also one of those simple tasks that can result in a complete mess of an otherwise pristine model if the wrong adhesive is used on a bad day.

A preserved Class 33 locomotive is displayed at an open day in a BR sector livery from the late 1980s complete with nameplates, depot plaque (far cab) and cast BR double arrows. All of these embellishments, which do much to make railway locomotives attractive, can be fitted by the modeller to almost any model.

'Galloway Princess' is a Class 47 locomotive in regular mainline use with Direct Rail Services (DRS) at the time of writing. Nameplates add something unique to the identity of a model as well as a full-size locomotive.

While most manufacturers simply print the plates, Bachmann goes one stage further with its regular releases of diesel locomotives by including etched nameplates with the model where appropriate. They are designed to be placed over a printed one on the side of the locomotive, giving the modeller the choice of using them or not, though most of us prefer to use them because they look so much better. If you have never tackled any detailing job on a model before, this might not be the best one to start with. However, it seems a shame not to use etched nameplates when they are included with the model. Also you may wish to renumber and rename a loco, even if it's not repainted, and fitting new nameplates is part and parcel of that process (see Chapter 5). Before you make a start, have some photographs of your chosen subject to hand in order to help with locating nameplates. For whatever reason you wish to add plates, this is how it is done:

1. Place the model on its side on a soft surface and tackle one side at a time. Leave sufficient time between each application for adhesive to dry before turning the model over to do the opposite side.
2. Do not use superglue, epoxy glue, impact adhesive or solvent cement to apply nameplates. It is possible to use PVA glue if it is diluted approximately 1:1 with water. PVA glue will dry clear but may not be strong enough nor be sufficiently viscous to stay where you need it on the rear side of the plate during its application.
3. Experienced modellers use varnish. To be more precise, matt enamel varnish that can dry to form a surprisingly strong bond between the nameplate and model. It dries clear, forms a really thin coating and offers sufficient time for adjustment before it sets. Usually varnish will not run when it is used straight from jar or tin, although it is not advisable to stand the loco up until the varnish has dried or there is a chance that the nameplate will slip through the effects of gravity.
4. Cut the nameplate from its fret and gently file away traces of the etched tabs until the edges of the plate are smooth. Check that it is flat.
5. Turn the plate over so it is face down and gently roughen the rear surface to provide a key for the varnish to form a strong bond to the metal.
6. Holding the nameplate in a pair of tweezers, apply a thin coat of varnish to the rear surface with a paintbrush. Do not flood it.
7. Transfer the nameplate to the model and drop it precisely in place. If you miss and make a mess, quickly remove the plate, clean off the varnish with thinners and try again.
8. When you are happy with the position of the nameplate, gently remove any excess varnish

Ready-to-run models often come supplied with nameplates printed in place. Some manufacturers will include nameplates in the box for the modeller to fit themselves. This picture is of a Bachmann Class 37 dressed in BR Coal Sector livery and would be fitted with a cast double arrow plaque located at (A) and a nameplate (C), which may be topped by a small plaque (B) if appropriate. This particular name is a commercially inspired one to please a freight customer.

from around the edges with a tissue soaked in thinners or a paintbrush similarly loaded with a small amount of thinners. Capillary action will draw the excess varnish away.

9. That's all there is to it. Leave the varnish to dry for a couple of hours before moving the model.

So, why not use CA glue? It would save a lot of time, and very experienced and confident modellers do use CA glue because it is quick and provides a very strong bond. That's all very well, but as you may gather from the technique described above, one false move and glue could get onto parts of the model where you do not wish to see it. Place the nameplate incorrectly and a clean-up is nearly impossible to achieve. It's not worth the risk on a £90 model.

When you have successfully completed an enhancement job such as fitting plates and plaques, it won't be long before you are tackling others. That said, adding etched nameplates to any named locomotive is a very effective way of starting to add enhancement detailing.

Some names, such as this fitted to GBRf Class 66, 66 702 (a Bachmann model) may be inspired by a railway tradition of celebrating the power of the machines themselves, nothing more.

Names may be applied to celebrate the services of railwaymen. This is a detailed ViTrains Class 47 detailed and finished as 47 739 'Robin of Templecombe'.

The real Class 47, No. 47 739 displaying its nameplate and plaque.

Part of the National Collection, 'Oliver Cromwell' (70013) is preserved in mainline condition, so its proud heritage and name can be seen all over the British (Network Rail) network today.

The simple cast metal nameplate applied to Class 33, No. 33 002.

Foster Yeoman, the Mendip-based quarrying company, named some of its small fleet of Class 59/0 locomotives with names to illustrate the corporate capability and strength of the company. 'Yeoman Endeavour' is the name applied to 59 001 and the name has survived numerous repaints of the locomotive. Some locomotives carry their plaques for many years and lifelong 'namers' are common.

A close-up of a double arrow plaque, available as an etch for modellers to fit to models painted in appropriate liveries.

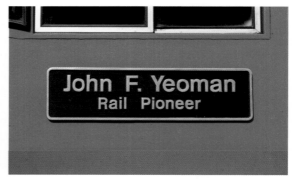

DB Schenker (formerly EWS) sometimes celebrates the achievements of railwaymen and people whose efforts have had a positive impact on the rail industry by naming locomotives after them, as was the case in the naming of No. 59 206 'John F. Yeoman'.

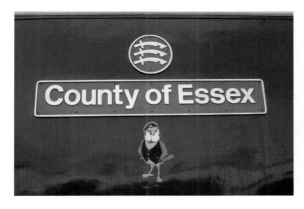

Names based on geography are still common, as seen applied to preserved Class 47, No. 47 580. It is common to see the names of counties, cities and towns, such as 'County of Essex' or 'City of Carlisle'.

Steam locomotives have their share of 'namers' for enthusiasts to follow and nameplates can take many different forms, as seen on 'Rebuilt' Bulleid Merchant Navy Pacific locomotive No. 35005 'Canadian Pacific'. The names for this class of locomotive were chosen from Merchant Navy ships of note.

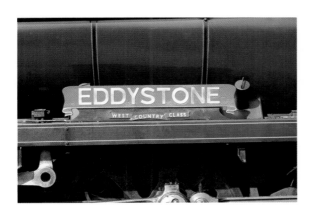

LEFT: 'Eddystone' is West Country Class 4-6-2 locomotive No. 34028, showing the nameplate style typically fitted to this locomotive class. Note the styling and the smaller plaque underneath. This type of nameplate can be obtained commercially for modellers to fit to the Hornby model.

BELOW: It is not unusual for certain steam era naming traditions to be carried forward to modern traction. First Group used Great Western Railway-style plaques on its Class 57 locomotives to bear the locomotive number instead of vinyl numerals, which adds character and variety. This photograph shows the Bachmann model of an FGW Class 57, complete with names and number plaques printed in place. Etched ones were supplied in the box.

Bachmann provides etched nameplates with most, if not all, of its diesel locomotive releases in OO gauge, such as its Class 37 model.

While Bachmann prints nameplate detail onto the side of its models, the etched plates are designed to fit over the print so it is completely hidden.

Further examples of plates supplied by Bachmann are those for its Class 57 models, including representations of cast number plates for the First Great Western Class 57/6 model.

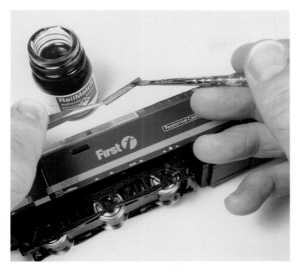

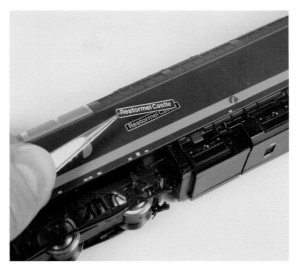

After cutting the plate from its etched fret, roughen the rear surface and then apply a thin coat of enamel varnish.

Carefully manoeuvre in place with tweezers. If you slip, cleaning up is easy with paint thinners.

LEFT: *Etched nameplates have more relief than printed ones, as can be seen on this Freightliner Class 57, which is a detailed and weathered Bachmann model.*

BELOW: *This is the Class 57/6 in First Great Western colours after fitting both nameplates and number plates. This is a feature adopted to mimic the old Great Western Railway tradition of applying locomotive numbers on its steam locomotives in the form of cast plates.*

ABOVE: **Naming ceremonies and rededications are the stuff of open days at depots and railway workshops. Class 73, No. 73 142 is rededicated at the Eastleigh Works centenary event in May 2009.**

LEFT: *An interesting variation on the nameplate theme is to detail a locomotive with a name board to identify a named train or a special service such as the Great Britain tour train, which tours Britain nearly every year. 7MT No. 70013 'Oliver Cromwell' was operated on the 2010 tour, 'The Great Britain III', which was photographed on the Aberdeen–Inverness leg of the tour at Forres, Morayshire, with name board attached. Name boards for famous trains of the past can be purchased for use on OO gauge models.*

DCC-READY AND DCC-ONBOARD

While on the subject of factory-supplied parts, note should be made of another area that requires the attention of the modeller before the model is put into use. The subject of Digital Command Control is generally outside the scope of this book, but note should be made of available 'DCC-ready' and 'DCC-onboard' locomotive models. DCC-ready is a misnomer in that it only indicates that a model is fitted with an 8-pin DCC interface socket called a NEM652 socket, the design of which follows the details set out as a standard in the NEM recommended practice published by MOROP (European Union of Model Railroad and Railroad Friends). NEM stands for Normes Européennes de Modélisme ('European Modelling Standards'). Like the National Model Railroad Association (NMRA; see Chapter 3), MOROP helps to determine standards and recommended practices to ensure reasonable interchangeability between manufacturers' models.

The socket enables the simple plugging in of a decoder fitted either with a harness and an 8-pin plug or a direct plug-and-play decoder with the pins an integral part of the circuit board. As the 'DCC-ready' expression incorrectly suggests, the model is not supplied equipped with a digital decoder: it is up to the modeller to source and pay for a suitable decoder. Once the decoder has been purchased, it usually takes a few minutes to fit a decoder to an 8-pin DCC interface socket and most ready-to-run UK outline models now have one.

To enable operation on analogue layouts, the DCC socket is fitted with a dummy bypass plug. This is removed to enable the decoder to be fitted, with the plug orientated so the pin connected to the orange harness wire plugs into the correct side of the socket. It is usually marked as pin No.1. Particular care is taken so the decoder does not touch any bare metal, which may cause a short, and that the decoder is not wrapped in insulation tape. To prevent accidental contact with metal, the offending metal surface is covered with insulation tape instead. With the decoder fitted and working satisfactorily, the dummy plug is safely stored away in the model's box in case it is needed again.

Some models, particularly from Bachmann, are equipped with a 21-pin interface that requires either an adapter to accommodate an 8-pin harness decoder or a special 21-pin direct fit decoder. Bachmann is at pains not to mark its boxes as DCC-ready but uses the symbols 8-DCC or 21-DCC to indicate the type of interface included in the model. A decoder of the appropriate interface will need to be purchased to fit the model and the dealer should be able to advise on suitable decoders.

Moving up the scale, there are those models marked as DCC-onboard. That is straightforward enough in that there is a factory-installed decoder inside the model. It will be ready to go on a digital layout on address 03 as supplied from the box. Read the leaflets on the decoder supplied with the model to check it is also analogue-enabled and how to change the address and other parameters to suit your operating conditions.

The high end of DCC-onboard locomotives are those factory fitted with digital sound decoders. The box will be clearly labelled and the legend usually says 'Digital Sound' or something like that. Again, the leaflets should provide a clear understanding of how the locomotive operates with sound and how to obtain the best from it.

In all cases, a decoder will not improve the performance of an ailing model. That is why the processes of running-in described in the last chapter and the maintenance routines described later in the book are important. Ensure the locomotive runs smoothly before installing a decoder. For more information on the fitting of digital decoders without fuss or burning them out, and for a comprehensive guide to decoder types and installation, please refer to the present author's book *A Practical Introduction to Digital Command Control for Railway Modellers* (The Crowood Press, 2008).

Models equipped with DCC interface sockets are increasingly common, either with the 8-pin socket or the more recent 21-pin interface seen here. In the case of 21-pin sockets, either a special adapter is required to use 8-pin decoders or 21-pin plug and play decoders can be used.

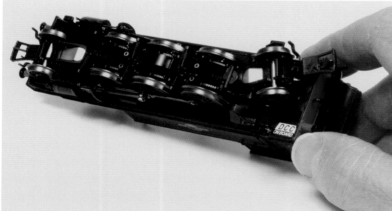

A Bachmann 'Prairie' tank locomotive fitted at the factory with a decoder. It is identified by a label on the underframe that reads: DCC Onboard. It will be ready to go on a digital layout on address 03 as supplied from the box. A separate leaflet in the box explains the workings of the decoder.

The internal arrangement of a typical DCC-sound onboard model. It's a Bachmann Class 37 fitted with a 20 × 40mm speaker and a 21-pin DCC sound decoder, both of which are fitted at the factory. The box is clearly marked 'DCC Sound'.

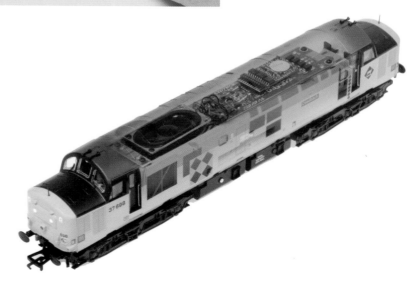

NEM COUPLING POCKETS

The final feature that falls under parts for fitting by the modeller are tension lock couplings designed to fit NEM coupling pockets for OO/HO gauge. They may be found in the bag together with the add-on parts, if supplied. The end of the coupling moulding is equipped with a fishtail connector that plugs neatly into the coupling socket, which may be fitted either to the frame of the model or the bogies.

The size and height of the NEM pocket is determined by NEM standards once again.

NEM362 (Boîtier pour tête d'attelage interchangeable, 'standard for interchangeable coupling heads')

in effect specifies the height, size, depth and shape of coupler boxes, so that couplings can be easily interchanged, provided they have the fishtail-shaped clip in the opposite end. The standard is absolute, with no room for interpretation, which is understandable because couplings must be standardized in order for them to work.

NEM362 coupling pockets have an important impact on the choice of couplings for British Outline stock because Kadee, the US-based coupling manufacturer, offers its world-famous buckeye coupling with NEM362 fittings in four lengths of shaft (Nos. 17 to 20), which clip directly into the coupling boxes at the correct working height for use with its range

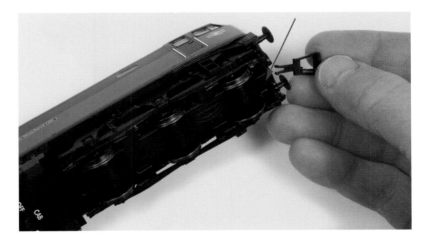

NEM362 coupling boxes can be moulded into almost anything: bogies, headstock locomotive frames and close coupling cams. This view shows a Bachmann Class 47 with a NEM362 coupling box moulded as part of the bogie frame.

A different bogie-mounted NEM362 coupling box mount, this time on a Heljan model and fitted with a No. 18 Kadee coupler, a NEM compatible version of the famous Kadee coupler.

of delayed-action uncoupling magnets. They are fully compatible with other couplings for HO/OO scale in the Kadee range and are compatible with the Kadee No. 205 height gauge. Kadee couplings offer dramatically more authentic operation even if the design is not strictly British. They enable delayed-action uncoupling and better performance than the tension lock type.

NEM362 pockets also accept another design, the well-regarded European close coupling (also known as the Roco close coupling). Hornby's own version of the same European coupling also works very well indeed, being both reliable and very cost effective to use, if a little bulky in appearance.

All of these features rely on the coupling box being fitted to the specified height by the manufacturer to deliver all of the operational benefits and, unfortunately, they do not always get it right. In those cases, the coupling boxes are removed from the model if an alternative coupling type other than

NEM362 coupling boxes fitted to the frame of a Hornby Class 08 shunter. Note that the box is fitted in turn to a NEM363 coupling connection. The advantage of this type is that the coupling box can swing slightly from side to side. On the downside, the NEM362 box can and will drop out of the NEM363 connection when in service.

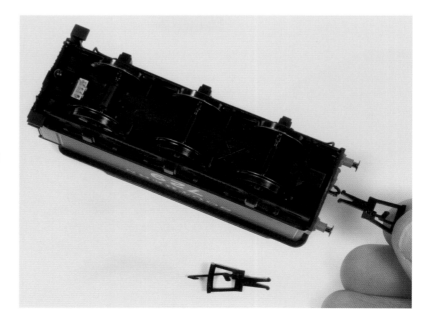

The Hornby T9 steam locomotive is fitted with NEM362 boxes on the tender and the front of the engine too. Note the fishtail end of the plug in coupling, a feature common to all NEM362 compatible couplings including the No. 17 to 20 Kadee couplers and European close couplings.

The NEM362 coupler box is frame mounted in a similar way to so many other locomotives. Note how the tension lock coupling supplied with the model clips neatly in place but is very easily removed.

Mention is made in this chapter of the European style close coupler. These are usually made to be NEM362 compatible, as seen in this shot of a Hornby version fitted to the Hornby T9 tender. Simply pull out the tension lock coupling and plug in the replacement.

the supplied tension lock coupling is required. When manufacturers get the height wrong, they frequently compensate by supplying a 'stepped' coupling that accommodates the mistake, so be alert to that.

Note should be made of NEM363, which is another coupling standard for HO scale models and adopted only by ViTrains for direct fitting of couplings. The coupling attachment is of a different shape and the fishtail-ended couplings used in NEM362 coupling boxes will not be compatible. Some separate NEM coupling boxes are designed to suit this connection,

but why this second 'Impérative' standard is seen as important is unknown and it is seen as unnecessary in the face of the NEM362 standard.

With the add-on parts fitted, couplings chosen and working satisfactorily, we can take a closer look at the all-important wheels. The next chapter looks at the different gauges that apply to 4mm scale modelling, problems that may be encountered with wheels and how to upgrade models with new wheels to both improve their appearance and performance.

CHAPTER THREE

LOCOMOTIVE WHEELS

The wheels upon which our locomotives and rolling stock rely are so vital but often taken very much for granted. Yet they can cause many different problems with reliability and can make or break a model if they are of poor quality or poorly maintained.

INTRODUCTION

Wheels are a fundamental part of a working model railway, in both rolling stock and locomotives. Strangely enough, they are very much taken for granted; yet if you are unfortunate enough to own a model with wheels that are out of true or have inaccurate back-to-back measurements, the performance of the model is greatly impaired in terms of its ability to haul trains, collect current from the track and to travel smoothly. Furthermore, wheels, like couplings, can cause a great deal of heated debate between modellers, especially when it comes to the choice of gauge within 4mm scale modelling, thanks to a historical compromise perpetuated today by the mainstream manufacturers: 4mm scale models riding on what is in effect HO scale mechanisms with wheels gauged to 3.5mm/ft (1:87.1 scale). Most modellers are used to this compromise and, for the sake of a quiet life, prefer to ignore it in order to have an operating model railway.

As a result of this scale-to-gauge compromise, wheel profiles or contours used on off-the-shelf British outline stock increasingly follow the recommended practices laid down by the NMRA (National Model Railroad Association; www.nmra.org) of North America for HO scale wheels because those practices have been established for a long time and are seen to be very workable. Wheels are increasingly referred to as RP-25/110 or RP-25/88 by manufacturers when they describe the features and benefits of their equipment. The codes refer to the profile of the wheel compared to NMRA recommended practices in document RP-25 (www.nmra.org/standards/sandrp/pdf/RP-25 2009.07.pdf). An RP-25/110 wheel has a deeper flange and wider tyre than an RP-25/88 wheel, which is more commonly used in closer-to-scale wheels and track such as finescale OO and EM gauge.

P4/S4 gauge is a more specialized area of scale modelling in 4mm scale that is intended to correct the compromise with British outline stock by fitting correctly scaled and gauged wheels. Like EM gauge, Scalefour models are not produced as off-the-shelf models by the mainstream manufacturers, which prefer to stick with the historical 4mm scale, OO gauge compromise because track is readily available for OO gauge (using the same HO scale track standards). Scalefour modelling has its own standards, which are published by the Scalefour Society in its digest sheet No. 1.2 (available at www.scalefour. org/resources/1-2v2-4.pdf). Modelling in this scale, even with off-the-shelf models, requires the use of new wheel sets to 18.83mm gauge.

For the record, EM gauge is also an attempt to achieve a correction to the scale and gauge compromise in 4mm scale models produced for the British market. Gauged at 18.2mm and with considerably easier wheel profiles (RP-25/88 is commonly used today) it is a very successful and workable compromise between the true 4mm finescale as promoted by the Scalefour Society and off-the-shelf OO gauge. Many modellers, including myself, opt for EM gauge as it gives the correct appearance of track gauge (OO/HO gauge track with 4mm scale models can look too narrow to many modellers' eyes), yet has more tolerance than Scalefour standards. More information can be found at www.emgs.org, including details of EM gauge track and wheel standards.

With the use of standards and recommended practices for wheels fitted to ready-to-run models comes the common compatibility of equipment between layouts of the same scale and gauge making life so much easier for the modeller to share locomotives and rolling stock with friends, to enable modellers to take trains round for use on a friend's layout during an operating session and to have the knowledge that equipment from manufacturer A will run with equipment from manufacturer B.

The NMRA established standards for wheels in 2009, including OO gauge, and those standards are now published on the NMRA website (www.nmra. org/standards/sandrp/pdf/S-4.2 2010.02.24.pdf).

Having established both the importance of wheels and the passions that arise from the choice of them, this chapter is dedicated to them: both those fitted at the factory to OO gauge and replacement wheel

sets for the closer-to-scale modeller working in OO finescale (16.5mm gauge), EM gauge (18.2mm gauge) and P4/S4 (18.83mm gauge). For the record, OO gauge (1:76 scale) wheels are basically the same as HO scale (1:87 scale) wheels, and the track gauge of 16.5mm is also the same, even though the bodies fitted to British outline stock are to 4mm scale.

TYPICAL WHEEL PROBLEMS

Wheels can cause almost as many operating problems as there are different types of locomotive wheel. Some of the common problems include:

- Dirty wheels preventing efficient current collection.
- Poor contact between the back of the wheel and current pickups.
- Dirt on the rear face of wheels.
- Pickups misaligned on steam locomotives so they catch the wheel spokes.
- Damaged traction tyres resulting in uneven running and poor haulage performance.
- Binding on steam locomotives and diesel electric shunters with coupling rods.
- Out-of-true wheels.

CLEANING WHEELS

Examine the wheels of locomotives (and rolling stock) to see how much dirt has accumulated on them. Wheels very quickly build up a layer of grime that can, in the finer scales, actually cause derailments as the effect of a finer flange is further reduced by dirt. Dirt also causes irregular running, interrupted power supply to decoders, flickering lights and poor sound reproduction from digital sound decoders. The overall effect is awful on a layout as the models run erratically and spoils the enjoyment of layout operation.

I regularly use a fibreglass pencil to clean locomotive wheels, mindful that fibre filaments can get into the mechanism. Care is taken to remove them after cleaning is complete. I also use isopropyl alcohol (IPA) and a cloth to clean wheels bearing in mind that alcohol can cause problems on paint finishes if

It is difficult to achieve good running to match the good looks of contemporary standard models if wheels are not kept clean, and checked to see if they are to the correct back-to-back measurements and that current collection pickups are all in contact with each wheel.

it is accidentally spilled or gets into the wrong place. This is particularly true if the model has been finished with acrylic paints and varnishes. Some modellers like to use mechanical cleaning devices that use what in effect is a brass brush, which is applied to the wheels to quickly clean them. One such device, the Kadee 'Speedy' wheel cleaner, is ideal for cleaning wheels on ready-to-run locomotives straight from the box, which are more likely to withstand this sort of cleaning.

Another technique I employ on certain locomotives that would otherwise be awkward to clean, such as those with extended cranks and outside frame coupling rods, is to place a few drops of cleaning fluid on a lint-free cloth, place it over a piece of track and then to run the locomotive partly on the cloth so that the dirt is easily removed by the action of the wheels. To ensure all the wheels are cleaned, the locomotive is turned round and the same task is repeated in the opposite direction.

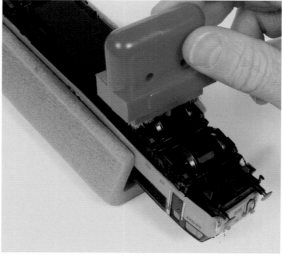

Many tools have been devised to provide a simple means of keeping locomotive wheels clean. This device is the Kadee 'Speedy' wheel cleaner, which has a dual action that applies power to the wheels, enabling the bristles to physically remove build-up at the same time as the wheels rotate.

Always take care when cleaning wheels on locomotives and rolling stock because the action is inherently aggressive. This may dislodge wheels on the axle, which can cause them to move out of gauge and may cause binding of coupling rods if the quartering of steam locomotive or diesel shunter wheels is moved out of position – even very slightly.

Another consideration, while on the subject of cleaning, is paying some attention to the inside face of each wheel where the current pickups make direct contact with the wheel for current collection. Dirt and fluff can accumulate here as well with the same loss of performance as if dirt had accumulated on the wheel tyre. IPA may also be used to clean both the inside face of the wheel and the pickups.

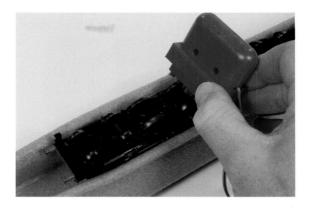

The Kadee 'Speedy' wheel cleaner can be used on all types of locomotive. It has several electrical connections so it can be used on one side only to avoid damaging traction tyres.

WHEEL BACK-TO-BACK MEASUREMENTS

Do not assume that any pre-assembled wheel set is set to the back-to-back gauge measurement of your chosen gauge – be it factory fitted to an off-the-shelf model or aftermarket wheels purchased from a specialist supplier. Of all the tools that are absolutely essential, the back-to-back gauge is top of the list. Check the wheel sets on your locomotives on a regular basis and those purchased before installation; and be aware that there may be a slight burr resulting from the turning of the wheel tyre, which could result in a false measurement.

As part of your ongoing maintenance of locomotives and rolling stock, it is worth checking back-to-back measurements of wheel sets regularly as they have been known to shift during use. The first signs of trouble usually arise when locomotives and stock start to derail in random locations on the layout. When this occurs, take a back-to-back gauge and carefully slide it between each wheel set. If the gauge is a tight fit, or cannot be inserted between the wheels, problems are inevitable as the flanges will strike check rails and will not travel through turnouts and junctions smoothly. The model will lift as it

Careful inspection of wheels and checking the back-to-back measurements ensures that locomotives and rolling stock will comfortably run through complex track formations without riding over check rails and switchblades.

Various gauges designed to check back-to-back gauging: the distance between the inner faces of wheels on a single axle.

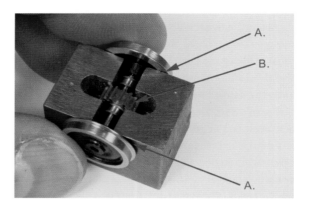

The gauge is placed between the wheels (A) on a single axle as shown here. Some gauges, such as this block gauge, have a slot (B) to clear a locomotive drive gear.

strikes check rails and could become derailed when wheels hit switchblades too.

If the gauge is loose or sloppy when inserted between the wheels, it too is out of gauge and this sets up different problems including a tendency to ride over the outer rail on curves and over switchblades too.

TRACTION TYRES

Traction tyres are a mixed blessing and can cause maintenance problems of their own. They wear out after periods of use and have to be replaced. As they wear, they become stretched and cause erratic

running of the locomotive. Replacements are generally made available from the manufacturers and can be purchased from stockists or spares specialists.

OUT-OF-TRUE WHEEL SETS

Diesel and electric locomotive wheels need to be perfectly concentric to prevent the locomotive running with a wobble or rolling motion made more obvious by the smaller diameter wheels fitted to such models. In both cases, the modeller relies on the manufacturer to achieve the correct gauge, wheel and flange profile in addition to perfectly concentric wheels.

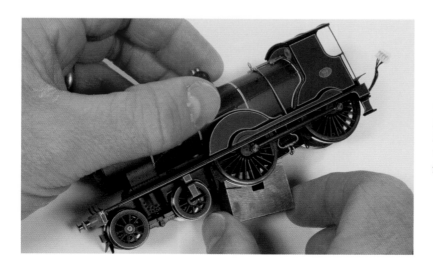

Routine wheel inspections will help prevent derailments by identifying out-of-specification wheels before they cause problems.

BINDING COUPLING RODS

For the benefit of readers who are newcomers to the hobby, quartering is something that is peculiar to steam locomotive building, where the opposing wheels on each axle have to be positioned so that the crank pins are positioned at 90 degrees (or a quarter rotation) in relation to each other. All of the wheel sets in a particular 'coupled' locomotive have to be quartered to exactly the same extent to prevent coupling rods from binding. To do this on the workbench requires a special quartering tool, or skill or a great deal of luck!

Sometimes, ready-to-run locomotives can suffer from moved wheels where the wheel rotates on the axle very slightly, moving the quartering and causing binding, which will result in jerky running. Remove the model from the layout immediately so the chassis does not become completely seized, causing serious damage or a burnt-out motor. Out of quartering is usually detected by careful examination of the model and determining which wheel is out of place. Do this by turning the wheels so the cranks on one side are vertical. Check the other side of the chassis to find which wheel is incorrectly positioned. Sometimes it is as easy as adjusting the faulty wheel back so all cranks are correctly quartered once again. Fortunately there is usually some slack in the coupling rods to allow for minute inaccuracies in quartering. If the problem persists after attention, a replacement wheel set should be sought and spares are usually available from the manufacturers, through specialist suppliers. Alternatively, return the model to the manufacturer for repair if such a service is offered.

Binding of coupling rods can occur even when quartering of the wheels is accurate. A coupling rod may be bent out of shape. Either bend it back or seek a replacement. The crank pin holes may be too tight and that can cause binding in some instances. Carefully open out the holes with a smoothing broach and refit to the model, applying fresh lubricant sparingly to the crank pins.

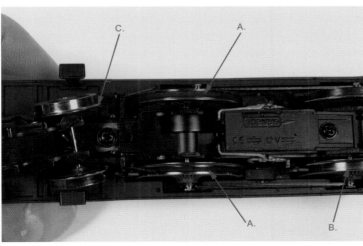

ABOVE LEFT: **Don't forget to check tender and bogie wheels of steam locomotives, not to mention unpowered bogie wheels on multiple units. Extend your inspection regime to wagons and coaching stock too.**

LEFT: **Traction tyres (A) are sometimes used to help lightweight locomotives get a grip on the rails. Not all driving wheels are fitted (B), so current can still be collected to supply the motor. Pickups are also fitted to bogie wheels of contemporary standard models (C).**

REPLACEMENT WHEEL SETS

As modellers seek either better running from their models, or conversion to either EM or P4 gauge, they frequently turn to replacement wheel sets. There is a wide choice of wheels and some research is required to find the correct ones to suit a given model. The correct axle diameter is important, as is the choice of wheel tyre material. Steel, nickel silver and brass are all popular metals for the manufacture of wheel tyres. Personally, I dislike steel because of the risk of corrosion. Nickel silver wheels can be more expensive than brass ones but are a popular choice nonetheless and I buy them whenever funds allow. Nickel silver is harder than brass and therefore less prone to wear. None of these metals has any particular advantage over the other, so it is very much down to personal choice and how much is available to spend.

Another factor to consider is the way in which current is to be collected from the rail. In the case of steam locomotive driving wheels produced by Markits, the modeller has the choice of how current is to be collected from the rails depending on the wheels chosen. Markits wheels are supplied either plain (live) or insulated. Plain wheels have no insulation between the wheel tyre and the axle, enabling current to be collected through the locomotive chassis frame on one side while insulated wheels are used on the other to prevent a short circuit. The other option is to use insulated wheels (where there is an insulating material between the tyre and wheel spokes) on both sides of the chassis, relying on wiper pickups to collect current and maintaining an electrically insulated chassis. This latter arrangement is preferred by DCC users and those re-wheeling ready-to-run models.

Other manufacturers' wheels have plastic spokes and centres, making them naturally insulated, so wiper pickups are required on both sides of the chassis, no matter which wheels are used. The method of current collection via the chassis and live wheels on one side of the chassis is now regarded as old-fashioned. Nonetheless, it is still practised, especially among locomotive kit builders, and modellers

need to carefully consider the impact of this practice on DCC decoder installations.

Finally, when building industrial shunting engines or converting ready-to-run steam locomotives with closer-to-scale wheels, check the wheel diameter of both bogie and driving wheels because there is tremendous variation in wheels, sometimes even within a locomotive class. Count the spokes too!

Manufacturers producing replacement wheels and conversion kits for British outline models include:

- Ultrascale (Gear Services Letchworth)
- Markits
- Alan Gibson
- Black Beetle
- Sharman Wheels

Modellers can choose from a variety of methods for re-wheeling ready-to-run models. The five generic methods for both steam and diesel electric models include:

Complete Conversion Packs. These consist of a complete set of wheels, axles, gears and bearings (also crank pins for steam and 'coupled' locomotives). They are usually fully assembled and may be fitted as a direct exchange for the original wheel sets. Some adjustment to pickups may be necessary to ensure a good fit, especially if OO gauge wheels are being exchanged for EM and P4 wheels where the distance from the back of the wheel is greater than with OO gauge wheels.

Ultrascale (Gear Services of Letchworth) has been a long-term supplier of comprehensive replacement wheel conversion packs for both steam and modern locomotives to OO, EM and P4 gauge. Markits also offers complete sets of steam locomotive class specific wheel sets including bogie, tender and driving wheels. The axles are self-quartering due to a square mount in the axle ends and the axles are available in a variety of formats including OO and EM gauge. The Hornby Class 08/09 shows the techniques for replacing wheels in coupled locomotives such as steam locomotives and the outside frame shunter as the techniques are basically the same.

Wheels Purchased Individually. Wheels are available with axles to the preferred gauge and the required diameter to suit the model for which they are intended. Markits offers different diameter axles to suit older models that do not accept the now commonly used standard $1/8$ inch diameter driving wheel axle. Individual locomotive wheels are also available from Alan Gibson and Sharman Wheels.

Economy Conversion Packs. These consist solely of wheels and axles, supplied unassembled, and offer a low-cost option, especially for diesel and electric locomotives. They have grown in popularity thanks to the increased use of 2mm diameter axles

and interference fitted final drive gears on diesel and electric locomotive models. The gears can be removed from the original wheels and reused on the new ones. Some conversion packs are designed to fit non-standard axles such as those on former Lima models fitted with new drives by Hornby as part of the reissue of the Lima range. Ultrascale is the biggest (indeed, almost sole) supplier of economy wheel conversion packs.

Turned Metal Wheel Sets. The use of individual turned metal wheel sets intended for rolling stock is on the increase. These are adapted for use in diesel and electric locomotive models by filing away axle pinpoints and reusing final drive gears

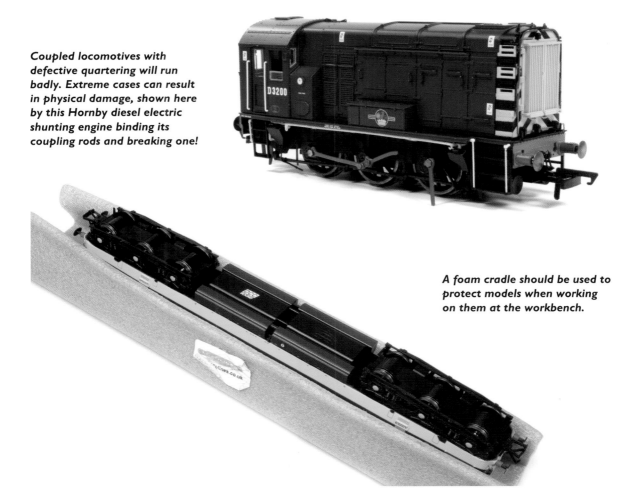

Coupled locomotives with defective quartering will run badly. Extreme cases can result in physical damage, shown here by this Hornby diesel electric shunting engine binding its coupling rods and breaking one!

A foam cradle should be used to protect models when working on them at the workbench.

recovered from the host model. Wheels produced by Markits and Black Beetle are suitable where the turned metal wheel is large enough for good contact between wheel and current pickups. The Heljan Class 33 project below demonstrates this technique.

Stub Axle Wheels. These are available as conversion packs for locomotives with split axles insulated by a plastic bush. The insulating bush may have the final drive gear moulded as part of it. Examples of such locomotives include the Hornby Class 31 and Hornby Class 50.

All manner of replacement wheels are available for equipping locomotives with closer-to-scale wheel sets.

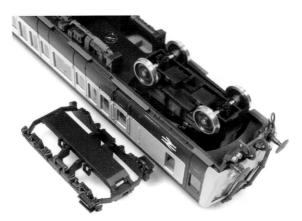

New wheels with brass tyres by Ultrascale are shown fitted to what was a Hornby Class 121 model (which has been converted to model a Class 122 single DMU car) using the original final drive gear recovered from the wheels supplied with the base model. Ultrascale offers economy or eco-conversion packs where it is left to the modeller to reuse the original gear, bearings and to make provision to current collection.

BELOW: *Back on the layout: the Class 122 tries its new wheels on EM gauge track.*

Steam locomotive wheels for kit builders and those wishing to fit closer-to-scale wheels to ready-to-run models; these ones are produced by Markits.

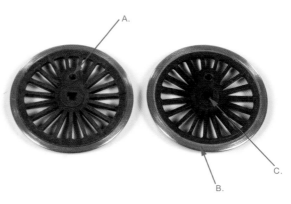

Most replacement wheels for steam locomotives are usually insulated. However, Markits wheels are supplied either plain (live) or insulated (there is an insulation layer between the tyre and wheel spokes) and have a square axle hole together with corresponding design of axle to aid quartering: (A) Crank pin mounting hole (threaded to accept Markits crank pins); (B) insulation layer between the tyre and wheel spokes on the insulated wheel; (C) square axle hole.

Basic tools and items for making up Markits steam locomotive wheel sets. If using wheels by another company, such as Ultrascale, which uses round ended axles, a quartering tool is also required: (A) Back-to-back gauge; (B) Markits axle nut and crank pin securing tool; (C) axles (usually $^1/_8$ inch); (D) crank pins; (E) crank pin securing washers.

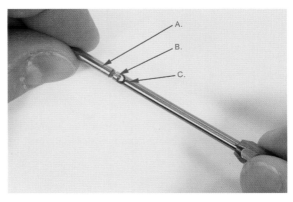

Using the axle nut tool: (A) Wheel axle; (B) wheel securing nut; (C) axle nut tool.

The axle is inserted into the squared hole.

The axle nut tool is designed to clear the middle of the axle like this.

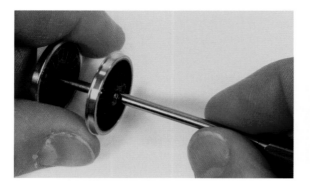

Tightening up: the square axle end and axle hole fixes the quartering of the wheel set.

The back-to-back measurement is checked – just in case.

The same tool is used to fit the crank pins, with the end of the crank pin being accommodated by the hollow end of the tool.

A complete set of driving wheels assembled and ready to use. Sometimes the design of a chassis means that the axle bushes are built into the frame, making it necessary to fit the wheels to the chassis, one component at a time, and not off the model as shown here.

WHY REPLACE WHEEL SETS?

There are a number of good reasons for using quality replacement wheels in OO gauge ready-to-run models that otherwise may seem to have perfectly good wheels straight from the box. The obvious one is a conversion to a closer-to-scale gauge such as EM or P4. Sometimes the wheels provided with a model locomotive are generic, bearing no resemblance to the wheels fitted to full-size locomotives. Changing the wheels can bring immediate and striking visual improvement to an otherwise mediocre model.

Many of the wheels fitted to off-the-shelf models are cast instead of being turned during manufacture. This presents several problems that may become apparent over time. Firstly, cast wheels are rough compared to turned wheels. Dirt can accumulate

in the minute imperfections on the surface of the wheel tyre, resulting in poor current collection and the need to clean them more frequently than would be considered desirable. Secondly, cast wheels cause a great deal more noise than turned ones when running at more than a low speed. Such noise is difficult to isolate, even with the use of cork and foam as track bed, and will have a bearing on the use of digital sound.

Choosing the most suitable wheels for a particular model is down to several factors. Firstly, does the model accept the closer-to-scale wheels or is the space between the bogie side frames too narrow to accommodate them? When this situation arises, the modeller is left with two choices. One action is to file excess material from the inside face of the bogie side frames of diesel and electric locomotives. The alternative is to rebuild the bogies so that there is sufficient room for the wheels. Steam locomotive operators may find that splashers and frames may be too narrow and require modification, particularly on older models.

Fortunately, nearly all up-to-date models can accommodate closer-to-scale wheels from OO finescale to P4 because models are finer, with better plastic mouldings and thinner bodies and frames. Things are made simpler as replacement wheel manufacturers either build in a boss on the back of the wheel to accommodate the side play that results from wider gauge wheels being fitted to an OO gauge chassis, a particularly important point with regard to steam locomotives, or offer suitable spacing bushes to pack the wheel sets to eliminate side play.

The choice of wheels may also be influenced by the diameter required to match the prototype. Most scale conversion packs are of the correct scale diameter for the locomotive for which they are intended. Sometimes, to save time and money, individual wheel sets such as those produced by Black Beetle can be used very successfully with diesel and electric locomotives, but at the small price of the diameter being slightly smaller than scale in some cases. I have successfully used Black Beetle 14mm diameter wheels in Heljan Class 33s and 47s to get them running on an EM gauge layout straight away. My excuse is the fact that tyres wear on the real machines. The reality is that the wheels are about 1mm too small in diameter for many classes, but they do work.

Full conversion packs produced by Ultrascale can save a great deal of time but cost considerably more than the purchase of an eco-conversion pack or individual wheels such as those by Markits. Full conversion packs are ideal for large steam locomotives with complex wheel arrangements because you get all that you need to complete the project, although they are rarely supplied assembled. Diesel and electric locomotive models with complex gear sets such as the old Lima Class 73s where the drive gear is moulded on the rear face of one wheel of each wheel set are the most difficult to re-wheel using straight wheel sets. Conversion

packs are preferred as they are supplied with the same moulded gear – the alternative is to cut the moulded gear off the back of the original wheel set and glue it onto the new one, a time-consuming and often precarious modelling task. Another situation that suits full conversion packs is the re-wheeling of the Bachmann or Hornby Class 08/09 shunter. The conversion packs for these locomotives include the outside frame cranks and bearings, making the job very simple to complete. Should I consider re-wheeling steam locomotives, it is worth paying the seemingly high cost of the wheels. Perhaps we take wheels for granted when, indeed, they are a vital part of a model and it's worth investing time and money in them.

GENERAL NOTES ON TECHNIQUE

Before starting work, buy or make a suitable locomotive cradle that will hold the model firmly when upside down on the workbench. This will prevent damage to the bodyshell and paintwork, as well as preventing the loss of standalone detailing parts. Failing that, clean the workbench top of all detritus from previous modelling sessions to avoid damaging the body. Dig out a piece of foam from somewhere to lay flat on the table.

Once you have bought your replacement wheels and are ready to fit them, do not be tempted to throw the old ones in the bin. Pop them in a poly-grip bag together with a label, so they can be identified, and then safely store them away. You never know how your modelling plans will change and a converted locomotive may not fit a future layout theme. Usually, in this case, resale beckons and being able to reverse the conversion and recover the scale wheels saves money and makes the surplus model more attractive to buyers not working in finescale modelling.

Body removal is not usually necessary to gain access to the wheels of most ready-to-run models. Study the instruction leaflet supplied with the model to locate screws or clips that hold the bogie baseplate in place. Usually a quick flick with a screwdriver or removal of two or three screws is all that is needed to release baseplate clips and gain access to the wheels. This is why a cradle is an excellent tool for holding the locomotive securely in the upside-down position.

Recovering the old wheels is usually as simple as pulling them free of the bogie frame. In the case of the Hornby Class 08/09, the middle axle has to be carefully manoeuvred from around the phosphor bronze pickup strip. With the wheels removed, and depending on which type of re-wheeling kit is being used, remove excess lubricant, look for unwanted foreign bodies and recover the final drive gear if using an eco-conversion pack. Don't forget to store the old wheels safely.

While the use of a full conversion pack is pretty easy, using an eco-conversion pack or individual wheel sets requires a little more care. In the case of an eco pack, fit the recovered final drive gears to the new axles. Centre them as accurately as you can before fitting the wheels. Bachmann locomotives have bearings that clip on to the bogie frame

of diesel and electric locomotives. These too should be recovered and reused. Check to see if there is likely to be excessive side play once the wheels are fitted to the bogie and, if that is the case, use spacing bushes to limit the side play on outer axles. It is worth having a little side play on middle axles of six-axle diesel locomotives.

Adjusting the pickups may be necessary on all models to ensure that they make contact with the rear face of the wheel, especially if the locomotive has been regauged to EM or P4. If there is a burr on the rear face of the wheel tyre, which may result from the turning of the tyre, this will interfere with phosphor bronze pickups, causing intermittent current collection and even some noise. Check for a burr and remove with fine grade wet and dry paper if necessary.

Colouring the wheels with paint, marker pen and weathering powders is necessary to blend them in

Two shunters at work: one is a Hornby model (nearer the camera), while the grey-liveried shunter is by Bachmann. Both can be re-wheeled with a conversion pack using the technique described in this chapter.

with the model. There is controversy surrounding this because wheel manufacturers rarely accept any warranty responsibility for wheels that have been chemically blackened or primed and painted by the modeller. This creates something of a conundrum for modellers who wish to have beautifully finished and weathered models with painted wheels to match a particular livery, such as an LNER express passenger locomotive. And that means that they have to be coloured or painted in some manner.

Check and run the host locomotive for a period of time to make sure that the wheels are satisfactory and performance meets expectations before applying any primer and paint, not to mention weathering, to the wheels. This means that you have the chance to check for faults and to return the wheels to the manufacturer in pristine condition before any paint comes anywhere near them.

Cleaning finer replacement wheels is an important part of achieving reliable running on the layout, as emphasized above. Scale wheels should be carefully cleaned to avoid abrading them excessively because the resulting damage will allow dirt to accumulate. I use isopropyl alcohol (IPA) as a wheel cleaner on scale wheels. More stubborn dirt can be removed with the gentle application of a fibreglass pencil when the wheels are rotating. Fibre pencils will burnish the wheels without causing excessive abrasion. Whatever you do, do not use wet and dry paper or a file.

PROJECTS

HORNBY CLASS 08/09 SHUNTER

Finescale wheels improve the appearance of this already lovely model and they are essential for modellers in EM and P4 gauge. This project shows the fitting of a complete Ultrascale wheel conversion pack where the wheels come supplied fully assembled, correctly gauged for immediate use on the Hornby Class 08 and 09, and fitted with outside cranks and pins as standard with the correct quartering. In effect, this project also demonstrates how

a replacement wheel conversion pack will work on a steam locomotive: the technique is exactly the same. The amount of valve gear that has to be dismantled will depend upon the model being worked on. One of the benefits of using this type of conversion pack for the Class 08/09 is that they are supplied 'quartered'. When assembling wheel sets this is sometimes difficult to do unless using wheels produced by Markits that have automatic quartering built into the axle fitting or through the use of a special quartering jig, which is recommended when assembling steam locomotive wheel packs.

One axle is equipped with a final drive gear that is an exact match to the gear train installed in the locomotive mechanism. This means that the drive gear on a Hornby wheel set does not need to be removed and reused. The Ultrascale wheels are supplied complete with crank pins, crank pin securing nuts and crank pin bushes. The crank pins themselves are an exact fit for the coupling supplied with the Hornby 08 shunter, so they may be reused.

Changing the wheel sets over is a fairly straightforward task. It is useful to have a few simple tools to hand including jewellers' screwdrivers, tweezers and fine lubricating oil. Some IPA may be useful for cleaning areas of the locomotive chassis if it has seen use in the past or to remove excess lubricant that may be present on brand new models.

First remove the body because it has many delicate components that can be easily broken if it is balanced on its roof, even in a foam cradle. Once the body is safely placed to one side, the chassis should be turned upside down so that the brake details can be unclipped. Undo the tiny crank pin securing nuts so that coupling rods can be recovered and placed to one side for reuse. Next, remove the wheel baseplate by releasing the three retaining securing screws and place that together with the screws in a safe place until later.

It is easy to remove the outer axles simply by pulling them free of the chassis. A phosphor bronze pickup assembly located over the middle axle has to be unclipped on one side so that the middle axle can be freed. All three wheel sets are refitted with the crank pin nuts and stored just in case the model has to be converted back. Excess lubricant and dirt are removed before the new wheels are installed. It is also worth taking a look at the current collection pickups to ensure that they are clean. Sometimes fluff, rail ballast and other debris make their way into a model mechanism if the model has been used regularly prior to the conversion. Seek it out and remove with tweezers.

In order to install the new wheels, the centre axle is carefully manoeuvred into place, once again lifting one side of the phosphor bronze pickup assembly and gently teasing the axle in underneath it and then into place. Ensure that the pickup assembly is clipped back into place before fitting the replacement outer wheel sets. The brass axle bearings must line up with the slots in the chassis and the axle fitted with the final drive gear is correctly positioned on the chassis so that the gear engages with the mechanism. If it is installed incorrectly, the wheel baseplate cannot be replaced because there is a recess to accommodate the final drive gear in the baseplate and that will not line up.

Before replacing the baseplate, ensure that all three wheel sets are fully pushed into place, that the current pickup wipers are acting on the rear face of the wheel tyres and that the wheels rotate freely. A small drop of oil may be applied to each axle bearing before the wheel baseplate is refitted to secure the wheels and pickups back in place. To see if this stage of the conversion has been successful, the model is placed on a test track and driven up and down a little to see that the wheels rotate freely before fitting the coupling rods.

Coupling rods

Hornby coupling rods do not need to be modified in any way to make this a successful conversion because the crank pins supplied with the wheels are machined to be an exact fit. The Hornby coupling rods can be easily broken if handled incorrectly and care needs to be taken at this stage of the conversion. Refer to photographs to make sure that the coupling rod pivot is correctly located towards the cab side of the centre axle.

Release the crank pin nuts on the new wheels, together with their crank pin bushes, and place them to one side. Slip each coupling rod in place, one at a time, and refit the crank pin bush together with a nut, tightening them carefully with your fingers. Once complete, test the locomotive again, looking for problems such as binding, clicking or any other sign that the model is struggling to run completely freely. My particular locomotive showed signs of binding in one place, and this was traced back to the centre axle crank pins, where the retaining nut was too tight. By loosening it by half a turn, the coupling rod was free to move on the crank pin and the binding problem was solved. Once happy with performance and confident that the coupling rods did not need to be removed for further adjustment, each crank pin nut was secured with a tiny quantity of Anacure Nutlock adhesive, applied with the tip of a modelling knife blade. The beauty of this material is that it is easy to release the nuts at a later date if required, yet the adhesive is strong enough to hold them in place during normal handling and operation of the model.

One of the problems with scale wheels of this type is that they are not supplied with the wheel balance weights that should be applied to each wheel on the opposite side to the crank, which is also the case with steam locomotive wheels. I cut some from thin slivers of nickel silver sheet using photographs as a guide to make templates. It should be possible to make them from 5 or 10 thou styrene sheet too, although they may catch other parts of the mechanism if too thick. I fitted the balance weights before reassembling the plastic brake rodding and brake-block assembly, taking advantage of the extra space to get this detail right. Trying to fit to these details with the brake assembly in place is much more difficult. That concludes the installation, just leaving painting and weathering to complete the picture. Refit the loco body and run in the model on a rolling road to check for faults as if it were a new model.

Hornby's representation of BR blue 08 528 was the chosen candidate for this conversion. This model will be partially repainted and detailed to represent a different member of the class for use on an EM gauge layout.

Ultrascale wheels are supplied fully assembled, complete with final drive gear, brass axle bearings, crank pins, crank pin nuts and bushes. In effect, they are ready to use and don't even need to be quartered on a special jig.

The locomotive body is removed, even though it is not essential to this conversion. This will save it from potential damage to the fine detail during handling when swapping the wheels.

When removing the body, do not forget to release the wire at the bonnet end of the locomotive that represents a wiring conduit pipe.

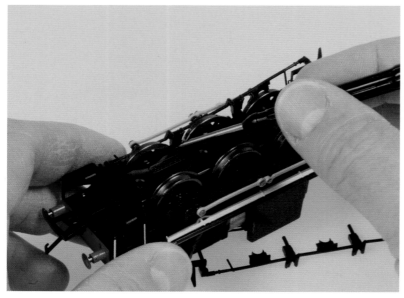

The next task is to remove the brake rodding and brake-block assemblies. They are easily teased out of the mounting holes with a jewellers' screwdriver. Avoid putting any pressure on the outside frames, coupling rods or wheels when removing the brake rodding.

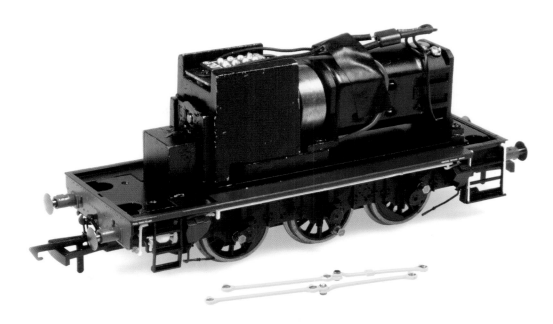

Coupling rods are removed by releasing the crank pin nuts, which should be replaced afterwards to save them if the Hornby wheel sets are stored for potential future use.

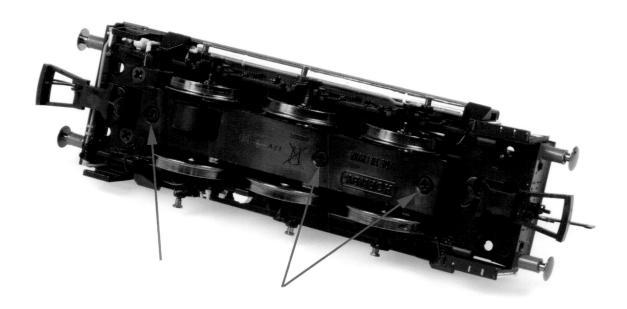

The three crosshead screws that hold the wheel baseplate in place can be removed with a jewellers' screwdriver.

Once the baseplate is removed, the axle and pickup arrangement is revealed. Note that the centre axle has a phosphor bronze current pickup assembly located across it.

While the two outer axles are very simple to remove, it is necessary to unclip the phosphor bronze pickup assembly on one side and tease the axle from underneath it.

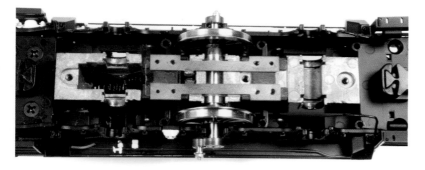

The middle axle must first be refitted carefully under the phosphor bronze pickup assembly before the pickups can be clipped back into place, ready for the simple installation of the two outer axles.

All three axles in place: note how the axle bearings clip into slots in the die-cast chassis frame. A small drop of lubricating oil is applied to each axle bearing before the baseplate is replaced. Surplus oil is mopped up with a piece of tissue.

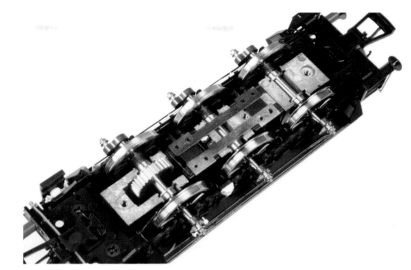

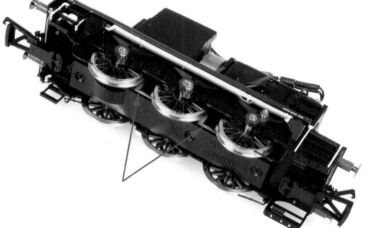

Check that all eight of the phosphor bronze pickups are making contact with the rear face of the wheels before refitting the brake rigging. Misaligned pickups will interfere with current collection and ultimately spoil the model's performance.

After thoroughly testing the model, it is advisable to use a specialist adhesive such as Anacure Nutlock or Loctite to secure them in place so that they will not become lost during normal operation, yet can be easily released for maintenance.

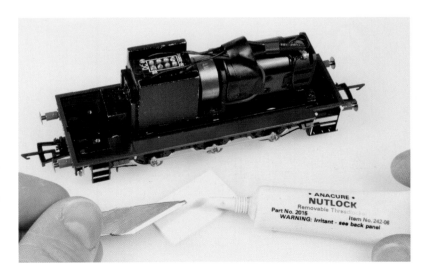

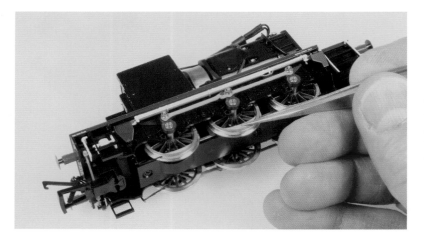

Wheel balance counterweights are not supplied with the conversion kit and should be made up and fitted to the wheels before the brake rodding assembly is reinstated.

Following the refitting of the brake rodding assembly, the model is checked again to ensure that the brake-blocks are not fouling the wheels. P4 gauge modellers will have to pay particular attention to this feature and be prepared to trim parts of the brake-blocks if they appear to be touching the wheel flanges.

The project is completed with the locomotive ready to operate on my EM gauge layouts. All I have to do is fit a set of Kadee couplers and it could go straight into use. The wheels, however, will have to be painted and the chassis weathered with rust and oil colours to represent working grime before this locomotive can make its debut.

HELJAN CLASS 33

The increasing use of 2mm diameter axles by manufacturers makes the re-wheeling of many models simple to do without having to resort to conversion packs, especially if the modeller is prepared to compromise a little on wheel diameter. A good example of this type of low-cost project is the Heljan Class 33 'Crompton' (the Class 26 and 27 also follow exactly the same format). A combination of 2mm diameter axles and final drive gears that are an interference fit to the axle makes this a good conversion to make a start on re-wheeling diesels.

There is a particular benefit in converting the Heljan Class 33 (including other locos in its range) because the original wheels are particularly rough castings and made of a relatively soft metal. I have noticed a distinct improvement in performance simply by replacing the wheels with 14mm diameter rolling stock wheels by Black Beetle. Turned in nickel silver, they produce less track noise when the model is being run and are also easier to keep clean. At 14mm in diameter, however, they are slightly undersize for a Class 33. The main benefit is that they are usually readily available and at a reasonable price too!

Heljan models such as the Class 33 are equipped with wheel sets with 2mm diameter axles. This makes a wheel replacement project easy to do with 14mm or 15mm diameter disc wheels or an economy conversion pack.

The conversion does not require the locomotive body to be removed. Simply turn it over and support it in a foam cradle. Unclip the four clips that hold the bogie keeper plate in place, two on each side. It is a bit of a struggle to jiggle the plate clear as one clip will pop back into place as the corresponding one on the opposite side is released. Once it's free, however, you will see that the wheel sets simply drop out ready to have the gears stripped off.

The new wheels are prepared by filing off the pin-points and removing one wheel, the one with the insulating bush, so the gear can be slid into place. It is a tight fit – tight enough that it grips the axle even when the model is working hard with a heavy train. Make sure it is centrally positioned before refitting the wheel to the axle and checking the gauge in a back-to-back gauge. Refit to the model, adjusting the pickups as you fit each wheel. No spacing bushes are required because the drive gear prevents axle side play, no matter the gauge chosen for the conversion. The bogie keeper plate simply clips back into place, holding the wheels and gears in place. Some oil may be required to lubricate the axles and the pickups may need further tweaking. No matter, this is as simple as a re-wheeling conversion can be in 4mm scale.

Heljan 'Slim Jim' Class 33/2 is the donor locomotive for a set of Black Beetle 14mm disc wheels, a very economical conversion for EM and Scalefour modellers.

It is easy to see why new wheels are desirable. The cast ones fitted by Heljan are rough and pick up dirt easily. New wheels will reduce running noise and will be less likely to collect gunge. To start the project, remove the bogie baseplate (keeper plate) by releasing the clips as indicated by the red arrows.

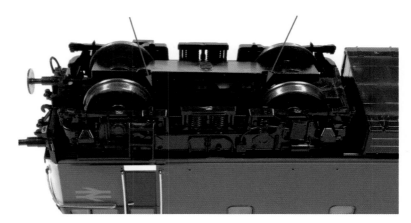

There's a lot of grease in those gears, perhaps too much. The surplus should be removed.

The design of the final drive gears (A) in Heljan locos means that wider gauge wheels such as EM and P4 gauge will not need any spacing bushes to reduce side play. The gears within the bogie frame will do just that. The pickups are also long enough to reach (B) the back of the new wheels and 2mm diameter bearing slots ensure that easily available wheels can be used (C).

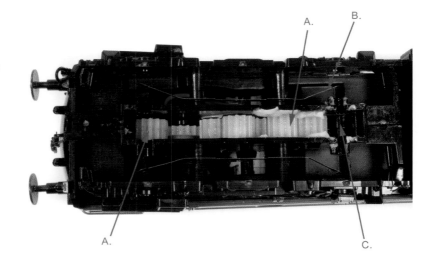

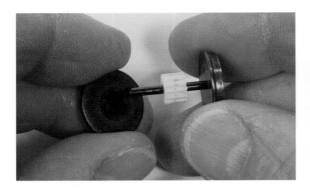

Dismantle the old wheels to recover the gear, which is to be reused.

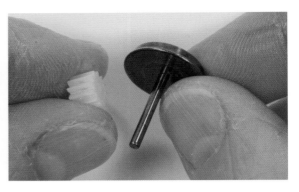

Handle the gears carefully so as not to damage them.

New 14mm diameter Black Beetle disc wheels, turned from nickel silver and gauged to EM gauge, were used for this project. The same approach applies for OO and P4 gauge.

The axle pinpoints are filed away since they are not required for this project.

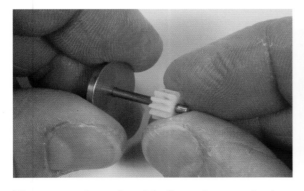

The recovered gear is a tight fit on the new wheel set axle, which is a good thing. Slide it into place until it is exactly centre to the wheels.

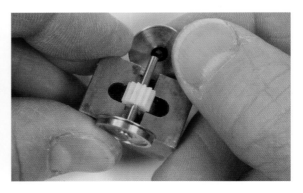

Assemble the insulated side of the wheel set, using a back-to-back gauge to set the correct gauge.

Drop (literally) the new wheel sets into the bogie frame. Note how the drive gears fill the inner space preventing unnecessary side play. The pickups are adjusted to touch the rear face of the wheels.

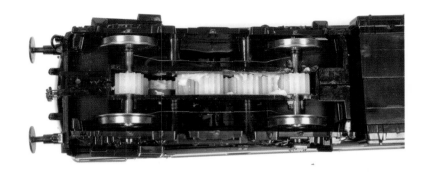

*BELOW: **Job done! The 'Slim Jim' Class 33 tries its new wheels on the author's exhibition layout.***

BACHMANN CLASS 37

This project describes the use of an Ultrascale conversion pack for the Bachmann Class 37. All of the wheel sets are supplied fully assembled and complete with brass gears and axle bushes. They are of the correct diameter for a Class 37 and are designed to drop straight into the model without having to use spacing bushes to prevent axle side play. If anything, they are slightly on the tight side.

As reported in Chapter 1, some Bachmann 6-axle drive models, including the Class 37, Class 47, Class 55 'Deltic', Class 57 and Class 66 have a largely irrelevant fault with their bogies. At least, it's regarded as irrelevant until the model is fitted with closer-to-scale wheels with a finer flange profile. The middle axle, together with its wheels, rides very slightly lower in the bogie (with the loco the correct way up), which means the bogies rock on the centre axle. The deeper RP 25-110 wheel profiles make this irrelevant to OO gauge layout operators. For the finescale modeller, the axle is adjusted by shaving 0.5mm of plastic from the inside of the hole that holds the axle bushes, levelling the wheels so that the bogie sits completely flat on the rails.

Once this simple adjustment is complete, the new wheel sets can be dropped into place, working each axle bush into its slot and clicking it into place. The pickups are adjusted to touch the rear face of the wheel and the bogie frames clipped back into place. Brass gears such as those used on the Ultrascale conversion packs may produce a little more noise than those moulded from delrin. Reduce the impact of this by using moly grease to lubricate them rather than fine model oil. Hob-e-Lube moly grease or its heavier gear oil will do the trick.

Class 37s are popular models and the Bachmann model, having gone through numerous improvements in recent years, is very popular among modellers. It makes a fine addition to a diesel and electric era layout, as seen in this picture of 37 698 on Dudley Heath Yard, my small exhibition layout and photo diorama.

An Ultrascale conversion pack for the Bachmann Class 37 comes complete with final drive gear and bearings. Apart from checking the back-to-back measurement (just in case), they are ready to drop in.

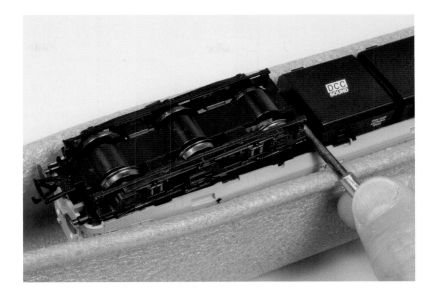

Remove the bogie side frame moulding by releasing the rear clip as shown.

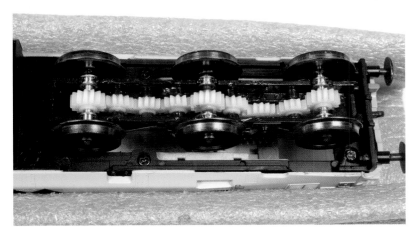

LEFT: *The original wheels are shown together with a tad too much lubricant, which should be removed to leave just a trace. Excess lubricant is a common problem with new models: even those that are not to be re-wheeled should be checked and the excess removed.*

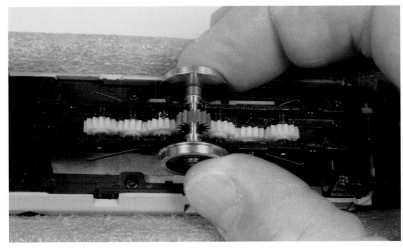

The new wheels drop straight into the Bachmann Class 37, with the frame bearings clipping neatly into the plastic bogie frame.

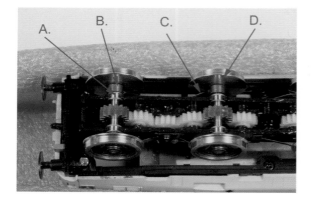

It takes only about ten minutes to complete this type of conversion from start to test run. The process is basically the same for the Bachmann Class 55, 57 and Class 66. Points to note include: (A) frame bearings that clip into the plastic bogie frame; (B) a plastic collar fitted to the rear of the wheels prevents excess side play; (C) current pickups are adjusted to touch the rear face of the wheel; (D) the rear face of the wheel is all metal with a smooth finish for good contact with the current pickups.

New wheels fitted and shown before the bogie side frames are refitted. The brass gears fitted to the axles may need grease or gear lube rather than fine model oil to complete lubrication of the model. The wheels will be primed and painted once running tests are completed.

There is no doubt that the Ultrascale wheels improve the appearance of the Bachmann Class 37 and this has to be one of the simplest conversions to undertake with a full conversion pack.

BACHMANN CLASS 55 'DELTIC'

The Bachmann Deltic can be easily re-wheeled with a conversion pack or individual wheel sets. It has standard 2mm diameter axles, which makes the reuse of its final drive gears, on either economy wheel packs that consist solely of wheels and 2mm diameter axles or 14mm diameter disc wheels, such as those sold under the Black Beetle name, simple to do – a very convenient arrangement that should be standard in all diesel and electric era models.

This conversion looks at using readily available 14mm disc wheels from Black Beetle (see above). They have the benefit of being turned from nickel silver, with a wide contact surface on the rear face for the pickups to touch for effective current collection. While they are supplied with 2mm diameter pinpoint axles, the points are easily filed away.

The original wheel sets are removed from the model by unclipping the bogie frames and pulling them free of the bogie frames. Bachmann uses brass axle bushes that are fitted to the axle. They clip firmly into the bogie frame and should be carefully teased out so as not to distort the frame. Strip out the wheel sets to recover the final drive gear and the bearings for reuse on the new wheels. Assemble them to the axles in the correct order and regauge the wheels in an appropriate back-to-back gauge before fitting to the bogie frames. The gear located between the bogie frames restricts the side play although brass bushing washers could be used to reduce any unwanted sloppiness. Remember that some of the Bachmann 6-axle drive locos have a small fault with the middle axle of each wheel. Check for this using a piece of glass and adjust before installing the new wheel sets.

Adjust the pickups so they touch the rear face of the wheel and refit the bogie side frame moulding frames, inserting each into the bogie frame front first before pushing it gently down onto the rear frame clip. When it clicks into place, the project is completed and the model can be test run.

The Bachmann 'Deltic' can be easily re-wheeled with a conversion pack or individual wheel sets thanks to the use of 'standard' 2mm diameter axles.

ABOVE: The 'Deltic' model is to be re-wheeled with Black Beetle individual 14mm disc wheel sets. These are turned from nickel silver and have a wide contact surface on the rear face for the pickups to touch for effective current collection.

RIGHT: A screwdriver inserted carefully at the inner end of the bogie is all that is needed to pop the moulding away to reveal the wheels.

With the bogie frame removed, working on both wheels and gears is straightforward. Bachmann uses brass axle bushes that are fitted to the axle.

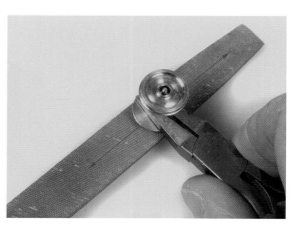

Individual disc wheel sets often come with pinpoint axles for use in rolling stock. The pinpoints are not necessary for use in the 'Deltic' and may be filed away like this.

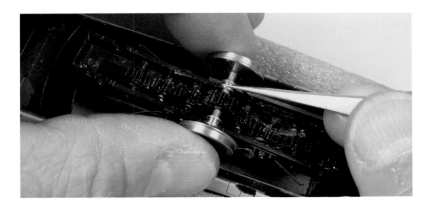

The new wheel assemblies are clipped into place and the pickups adjusted to touch the flat rear surface of the wheel. The original wheels are bagged, labelled and stored.

A.
B.
C.
D.

LEFT: *The Deltic's original wheels are dismantled to recover the drive gear and bogie frame bearings. This picture shows a comparison between an original wheel set assembly and a completed Black Beetle assembly with the recovered gears and bearings: (A) Black Beetle wheels are turned from nickel silver and are solid with no plastic centre; (B) the original bogie frame bearings are used; (C) some spacing bushes are needed to prevent excessive side play of the wheels when fitted to the bogie; (D) the original drive gear is an interference fit to the axle of the new wheel set.*

BELOW: *Care and attention to fitting the wheels together with realigning the pickups and checking the back-to-back measurements means this model will now run smoothly through complex track work without riding over check rails and crossing vees.*

BACHMANN CLASS 66

While this conversion is broadly similar to the Class 37 and 'Deltic' projects described above, I used an Ultrascale eco-conversion pack to convert this model to EM gauge. The process of removing the bogie frames and then the wheels to recover the gears and axle bushes is the same as that described in the 'Deltic' project. The difference is that the eco-conversion pack consists of correct diameter wheels turned from either brass or nickel silver with plastic

centres: 2mm diameter axles are supplied with the wheels that have to be assembled by the modeller.

Fit one wheel to each axle, ensuring it is not twisted, and slip on the axle bush, then the drive gear followed by the second axle bush before fitting the other wheel to the axle. Use a back-to-back gauge to check the gauge before moving to the next one. Once all six wheel sets are assembled, they may be fitted to the bogie frames as before, pressing the axle bush into the axle slot. Adjust the pickups before clicking the bogie frames into place.

This Bachmann Class 66 is fitted with a six-axle eco-conversion pack with nickel silver tyres as offered by Ultrascale. This type of conversion requires the recovery of the original drive gears and bogie frame bearings for reuse on the new wheels.

The wheels fitted by Bachmann are of reasonable quality and most OO gauge modellers may decide to retain them. Modellers working in finescale will see a benefit in replacing them with closer-to-scale wheels. They always seem to improve the appearance as well as the running of already superb models such as this one.

The difference between factory-fitted and scale wheels after conversion is well demonstrated here.

An Ultrascale economy conversion pack consisting of wheels and 2mm diameter steel axles was chosen for this locomotive. No gears and bearings are provided and the wheels are not supplied assembled.

Pop the bogie off by inserting a screwdriver in the back of the bogie frame to release it from the clip.

The wheel sets consist of final drive gears and brass bushes securing the wheels in the bogie frame.

The gears are not wide enough to prevent side play. Consequently it may be necessary to insert some spacing washers when assembling the new wheel sets.

The old wheels are dismantled to recover the gears and axle bushes for reuse. The old wheels are carefully stored away in case they are needed again.

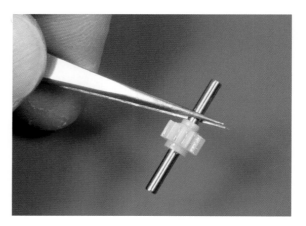

The drive gears simply slide into place on the new axles. The fit is tight enough for the gear to grip the axle, even when the model is under load.

LEFT: The completed wheel sets are checked in a back-to-back gauge: (A) smooth, turned nickel silver tyres; (B) there is a boss on the rear face of the wheels that helps prevent side play; (C) axle bush recovered from the original wheel sets; (D) additional washers for preventing side play, if needed; (E) the original drive gear recovered for reuse.

BELOW: New wheels without the bogie side frames refitted. It's worth testing a model like this just in case adjustments are needed. Notably, the phosphor bronze pickups are very visible. One refinement would be to paint them black or dark grey so they cannot be easily seen from behind the bogie frames.

In the case of heavy locomotives like the Bachmann Class 66, the use of smooth turned wheels has little effect on tractive effort. I have loaded up this particular model with very long trains without any sign of it slipping or being unable to start its train. Here it is seen working a relatively short train of ballast/spoil wagons during its first running tests after conversion.

HORNBY CLASS 31

Two models in the Hornby range are equipped with split-axle wheel sets composed of two stub axles with half-length axles that plug into an insulating spacing bush that also has the final drive gear moulded to it. Those models include the Class 31 and Class 50. The smaller Class 31 is featured in this project because, unlike the Class 50, not all of the wheels are of the same diameter. Of the six axles, which are all driven on this model, the middle one of each bogie should, to be prototypical, have a smaller diameter wheel set.

This project uses the Ultrascale conversion pack, which includes the smaller diameter wheels. The model can be worked on without having to remove the bodyshell because the bogie baseplates simply unclip from the bogie frame. The same baseplate also retains the bogie side frames, which can be removed when the baseplate is unclipped. The wheels are removed, noting that there are phosphor bronze pickups fitted to the inside faces of the bogie

side frames. The ends of each wheel set fit into the pickup strip just as the ends of a full-size locomotive axle fit in the roller bearings in the bogie side frame. Current is transmitted from the wheels, to the ends of the axles to the pickup strip.

The old wheel sets are removed and the wheels unplugged from the plastic spacing bush. The bush, together with its moulded gear, must be retained and reused, the new wheels being push fitted to it and the gauge checked with a back-to-back gauge, as before.

Each wheel set is refitted to the model – smaller diameter wheels to the middle axle position – and the ends of the stub axles aligned with the pickup strips. The bogie side frames are brought together with the bogie frame and the baseplate refitted to hold everything together. The same technique is used to convert the Hornby Class 50, although the wheels for that conversion are also produced by Black Beetle. Note that the Class 50 does not employ smaller diameter wheels, unlike the Class 31.

ABOVE: *The Hornby Class 31 uses split axles for current pickup through the axle ends. Conversion packs usually consist of half axles, as seen here. The original drive gears, which are also the spacing bushes for each wheel set, are recovered from the model and reused as part of the conversion.*

RIGHT: *A soft foam cradle protects the model while the wheel conversion is undertaken.*

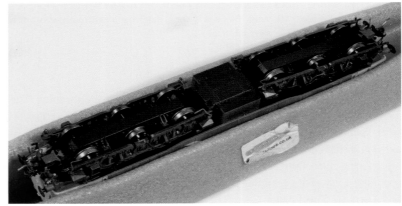

It is usually possible to remove the old wheels by releasing the bogie baseplate. Locate and release the clips gently with tweezers or jewellers' screwdrivers.

When the baseplate is removed, check for foreign bodies and excessive lubricant. This model has about the right amount of lubricant for reliable running. Note that the current collection method on the Hornby Class 31 is through contacts in the bogie frame (A) and the ends of the axles (B).

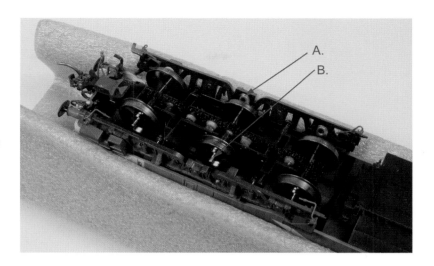

The original Hornby split-axle wheels as removed from the Class 31 and dismantled to recover the spacing bush and gear moulding.

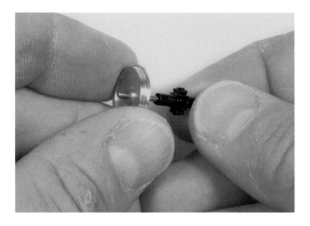

The new wheels are carefully plugged into the spacing bushes, which also include the drive gear.

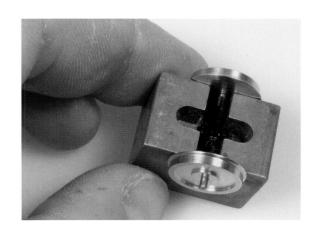

RIGHT: To be on the safe side, the assembled wheel and gear sets are checked in a back-to-back gauge. This block type has a slot that clears the gear, making it easier to do this task.

Note how the current pickups are arranged in this model: the ends of the axles fit the phosphor bronze 'axle boxes' (A), which means the bogie side frame spigots (B) must be clipped back into the bogie frame (C) when the wheels are dropped back into place and the baseplate replaced.

Dropping the completed wheel sets into place with the drive gear correctly aligned with those fitted to the bogie frame.

When undertaking the Class 31 conversion, remember that the middle axle wheels in each bogie are of a smaller diameter than the outer ones, so don't mix them up: (A) wheels have a solid rear face and no plastic centre; (B) the bogie side frames clip into the bogie frame and are secured with the baseplate; (C) note the alignment of the final drive gear so it engages with the gear tower train; (D) take care to engage the axle ends and current collection contacts properly.

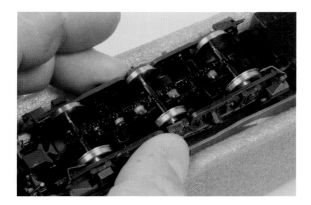

LEFT: *Gently squeeze the bogie side frames together with fingers until the spigots are tight in the bogie frame. Clip in the baseplate to hold it all together.*

MIDDLE: *The finished conversion. The wheels are a little bright, but nothing that priming and painting cannot cure.*

BELOW: *Into service with new wheels it goes! Test the model before undertaking priming and painting just in case there's a fault with the wheels. Some wheel manufacturers will not accept warranty returns if wheels are painted, primed or blackened.*

HORNBY CLASS 153 SINGLE-CAR MULTIPLE UNIT

To complete the picture is this model of a single-car Class 153 multiple unit, a new release by Hornby from 2009. The model does not use a die-cast chassis with centrally fitted motor and flexible shaft drive, but instead Hornby chose to utilize its short wheelbase drive bogie, which is also used in the re-issued Class 73, Class 101 DMU, Class 121 single-car unit and the Class 156. Only one motor bogie is employed: the other end of the Class 153 (and indeed the powered vehicles of the other multiple unit models) has an unpowered bogie with current collection pickups. This arrangement is more than adequate for the Class 153, which only has to power itself.

This particular technique using the Ultrascale conversion kit also applies to the Class 101, Class 121 and Class 156 models. Be sure to buy the correct conversion pack to ensure you have enough wheels for the two-car Class 156 and three-car Class 101 sets. The conversion pack follows the drop-in format of assembled wheel sets with a brass gear fitted to the axle for use in the power bogie and two wheel sets with no drive gear for the unpowered bogie. In both cases, the bogie frame is unclipped from the power bogie and the factory-installed wheels are removed. The new ones drop straight in and, thanks to the design of the Ultrascale wheel packs, do not need to

The Hornby Class 153, released in 2009, can be converted to EM and P4 using both full conversion packs and the less expensive eco-conversion packs from Ultrascale.

A single power bogie is fitted to the Hornby Class 153.

The opposite end of the vehicle has an unpowered bogie fitted with current collection pickups.

Starting with the power bogie, the wheels are removed by first unclipping the bogie baseplate.

A similar arrangement is to be found on many other models.

The wheels are removed and the current collection pickups adjusted so they will make contact with the new wheels: (A) drive gears; (B) phosphor bronze wiper pickups; (C) bogie frame clip – do not release unless needing access to the motor and gears.

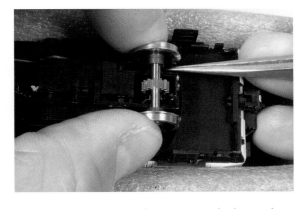

The complete new wheel sets are simply dropped into place. Complete conversion packs such as this come complete with brass final drive gears. Once fitted, the baseplate is reinstated.

BELOW LEFT: *The unpowered bogie is of a similar design, except there are no gears.*

BELOW RIGHT: *New wheels simply drop into place and the pickups are adjusted to suit.*

The job is finished except for painting the wheels to hide the shiny metal. The result is smooth performance through hand-built EM gauge track and quiet running.

be bushed. Pickups are adjusted and the bogie side frame moulding clipped back into place.

The unpowered bogie is treated in a similar manner; the simple retaining plate being unclipped from the bogie frame and the wheels removed, to be replaced by the new ones. Again, the pickups will need adjustment to ensure they touch the rear of the wheel tyre.

It is worth noting that there is an eco-wheel pack suitable for this conversion that involves the recovery of the original drive gears for reuse. The picture of the Hornby Class 121 (converted to a Class 122) in this chapter shows the same type of power bogie fitted with the eco-conversion pack.

CONCLUSION

While replacement wheels increase the cost of a model, something that finescale modellers factor into the cost of their locomotives anyway, the improvement in running performance and appearance makes them worthwhile. The main producer of diesel and electric locomotive wheel conversion packs is Ultrascale, a company with a long

delivery time, usually twelve weeks or more, so it's worth planning ahead to be sure you have the wheel conversion packs you need to hand or to consider individual wheels that may be purchased with minimal lead-in time. Steam locomotive wheels can be purchased from a greater number of suppliers with less lead-in time, unless the complete sets or individual wheels from Ultrascale are sought. When it comes to working with most diesel and electric locomotives, it is possible to explore the various turned wheels available from a number of manufacturers, including Markits and Black Beetle, to expedite simple but pragmatic conversions, provided there is room to allow pickups to make contact with the rear face of the wheel and the model's final drive gear will fit on the axles of the replacement wheels. Whichever way you go, the end result is, in my experience, very much worthwhile.

In the next chapter, refinement of drive systems and other technical aspects of locomotive models beyond the basic running-in and inspections are covered: everything from new motors to new current collection pickups and working cooling fans.

CHAPTER FOUR

MECHANICAL ENHANCEMENTS

Smooth operation on our layouts is the reason for spending time fine tuning and maintaining our model locomotives. Without them, we cannot run our railways! A Heljan Class 47 powers smoothly along the author's fixed layout with a mail train. It has additional current collection pickups and a sprung middle axle on each bogie.

INTRODUCTION

Something once fairly ingrained in British outline railway modelling was the huge amount of tinkering, fiddling, adjusting and beating about that was required to get very crude mechanisms, such as pancake style ringfield motors, to deliver some reasonable performance in order that our locomotives could put in a day's work on the layout. At one time ringfield motors were fitted to almost every OO gauge model produced by Lima, whether steam or diesel based. Hornby almost exclusively used ringfield motors in models produced in the late 1970s through to the introduction of the 'new generation' models that we enjoy today. Ringfield motors ended up in the tenders of steam locomotives and single bogie drive mechanisms in its diesel locomotives.

While Lima did nothing to upgrade its ringfield motors, Hornby did, as an interim measure, upgrade to five-pole armatures, which did much to improve performance. Nonetheless, current pick up from the track via the wheels was pretty minimalist on

older models, often relying on a current path from wheels on one side of the powered bogie, contact from the axle to the bogie frames and direct contact from there to the carbon brushes. The unpowered bogie had a similar arrangement, except for the use of a wire to connect the unpowered bogie to the body of the model, and then to the motor bogie. The result was inconsistent current collection and hesitant running, which could be easily solved by the addition of new pickups.

With the introduction of better-engineered models from Bachmann and Hornby has come improved performance, quieter running and much better control particularly at slow speeds. As new-generation models become available that match those available in Europe and North America for many years, modellers still experience some strange decisions in the way that the locomotive drives and electronics are designed. For example, Bachmann's first Class 37 model had a very strange unpowered and sprung axle on the inner end of each bogie, which meant the model was a four-axle drive affair of considerable power but with an unfortunate

All kinds of different solutions were sought to improve performance of older Hornby and Lima models. This Hornby Class 58 was fitted with a new frame motor for smoother performance. Heljan now offers a very good model of a Class 58 with a modern chassis and drive, eclipsing the ageing Hornby model.

As contemporary standard models began to appear, modellers sought to strip out drive components to upgrade other models that are much needed but long in the tooth. The parts from a Bachmann Class 25, for example, were often used to upgrade the old generation Hornby HST by replacing the ringfield motor bogie with a better drive.

tendency to sit down on the rear axle of each bogie when power was supplied, resulting in derailments. Fortunately Bachmann has corrected this design fault by introducing all-wheel drive mechanisms.

Another area where the new-generation models can be a bit lacking is in current collection from the wheels. While current collection is usually taken from all the wheels of a locomotive chassis, including the bogie and tender wheels of steam locomotives, that has not always been the case. Bachmann's first release of its Class 66 diesel locomotive only had pickups to the two rear axles of each bogie, which meant the locomotive effectively gapped itself over complex junctions, resulting in inconsistent performance. Some pickups are so fine that they could well wear out after prolonged running. In the case

of the Bachmann Class 08 shunter, for example, the current collection pickups actually worked on the tyre of the wheel rather than on the back of the flange. This resulted in dirt becoming trapped between the pickup and the wheel with the inevitable poor running.

Some models are still offered with fairly inadequate mechanisms for various reasons, mostly historical, as the model may have been available for many years with little or no upgrading. This chapter takes a look at some simple ways by which model mechanisms can be fine tuned to improve performance, new pickups can be added to ensure that locomotives do not lose contact with that all important supply of electricity, and ideas for improving models with completely new equipment.

A typical Hornby old-generation chassis with a single ringfield motor at one end and an unpowered bogie at the other. Note the minimalist ballasting of the model; often performance could be improved by simply adding another 150 to 200 grams of ballast to the model.

The same chassis with Bachmann Class 25 drive components fitted to it, demonstrating one technique for rebuilding older models. Since this conversion was undertaken, Hornby has re-released its HST power car model as a completely new tooling. The drive is a new-generation mechanism capable of considerable haulage power.

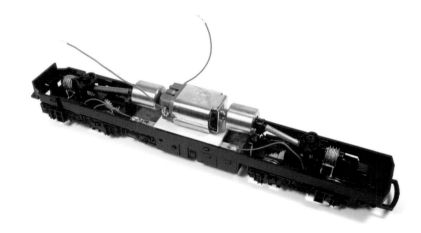

IMPROVING WHAT WE HAVE

Sometimes the only option available is to improve what we actually have to hand. Some modellers have decided to hold on to older equipment for a variety of reasons. These might be financial, for example when the funding is simply not available to replace older models with new ones with upgraded drive systems. Others may have put considerable time and effort into detailing and painting in order to make cosmetic changes to the model, an investment they are reluctant to dispose of. There are several models in my own personal collection (Lima

Class 73s) that fit the latter category; I simply do not wish to dispose of them and continue to use them regularly. To ensure that they remain reliable in the years to come, I have made small improvements to the pancake motor drive bogies, fitted additional pickups to the unpowered bogie and purchased a small number of spare motors so I can strip them for spares, such as carbon brushes and springs.

There are numerous options available to keep in service older models that are otherwise cosmetically acceptable. These include fitting a new five-pole motor, fitting additional pickups or even replacing the chassis in its entirety. When it comes to replacement chassis, ViTrains has made the chassis for its diesel electric locomotives available as complete running spares so that owners of older Lima locomotives can transplant the bodies, yet retain any cosmetic detailing improvements that they may have made to the older model.

The old Lima power bogie can be fine tuned using some simple techniques. The gears on the rear of the motor casing are removed and examined for burrs and moulding marks. These are easily pared away with a sharp modelling knife before reassembly to the motor casing. When the retaining spring is refitted, small brass washers are fitted over the gear spindles reducing the friction between the gears and spring.

The motor can be made to run much more quietly by using moly grease or white grease such as that sold under the Hob-e-Lube label. This is much more effective than one of the great myths of railway modelling, which was to use toothpaste in an attempt to quieten down the whirring noise that Lima pancake motors are famous for. Very little could be done to reduce this noise other than to tidy up the gears as suggested above. It was simply a characteristic of that drive bogie. Occasionally a squealing noise could be heard coming from Lima drive bogies that sounded fairly alarming and was an indication that the motor spindle itself was dry of lubricant. That problem was easily solved by placing a tiny drop of fine model oil on each of the motor spindle bearings that could be found either side of the motor casing. Finally, many modellers replace the thin, fragile wire between the power bogie and trailing bogie with something more substantial.

As new-generation models became available, many modellers looked into using components from them to upgrade older models that at the time seemed unlikely to be replaced by new versions. When Bachmann released its Class 25 model, it was heaven sent in that it provided competent drive bogies and chassis components that could be used on various other models, including the Hornby HST. For the record, that heritage model has now been replaced by a brand new version, making rebuilding of the old model unnecessary if you are prepared to discard it.

At the time, the motor, twin flywheels, drive shafts and bogie frames from a Class 25 could easily be transplanted into both Hornby and Lima HSTs, Lima Class 101, 117 and 121 DMUs, Lima Class 73s and a whole host of other models. Unfortunately the effort required for such conversions took a lot of time and involved additional cost that worked out at only slightly less than it now costs to buy a completely new-generation model. At the time of writing, many popular models from the former Lima range and those produced by Hornby remain to be upgraded with the very best of drive mechanisms, leaving the modeller with the task of transplanting drive components from locomotives like the Bachmann Class 25 in order to achieve the same level of performance enjoyed with new-generation models.

NEW PICKUPS

Fitting new pickups to either older models that don't have enough current collection capacity, or new ones where the pickups are fragile and easily damaged, is usually straightforward. All you need is phosphor bronze strip or 0.45mm nickel silver wire to make the sprung pickup, together with some method of mounting the pickup to the bogie or chassis frame. In the case of phosphor bronze strip, a popular method is to solder it to a piece of copper clad sleeper strip, which is, in turn, glued to the chassis frame in a location where it does not interfere with the wheels.

One of the advantages of using nickel silver wire is that it can be soldered to the head of slotted brass screws. Screws are easier to fit to a bogie or chassis frame than pieces of copper clad sleeper. Once the pickup is in place, it is simple enough to adjust it so it makes contact with the rear face of the wheel tyre. If it looks as if the pickup is likely to touch some part of the chassis frame where it would cause a short circuit, it is easy to thread a piece of insulation stripped from equipment wire along the pickup to prevent contact from being made. In the case of phosphor bronze strip, insulating it from accidental contact is not as easy and some modellers use liquid masking film normally used for painting for this purpose.

Another modern prototype modelled by Hornby: the Class 395 'Javelin' high-speed EMU.

It is possible to further improve this model with improved pickups. If re-wheeling to EM or P4, replacement pickups formed of nickel silver wire must be fitted because the factory-fitted ones will not reach the back of the wheels!

The unpowered vehicles can be upgraded to improve running by fitting pinpoint bearings. This is also a solution to repairing worn axle holes on plastic bogie frames. Commence by opening up the axle boxes with a 2mm diameter drill to a depth of 2mm.

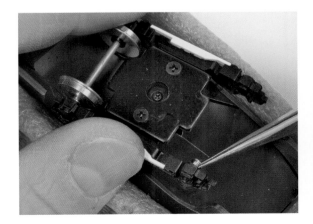

Insert 2mm diameter top hat bearings so they sit tight in the bogie side frames.

Refit the wheels. In this case, the original Hornby wheels have been replaced with closer-to-scale versions for operation on the author's EM gauge layout.

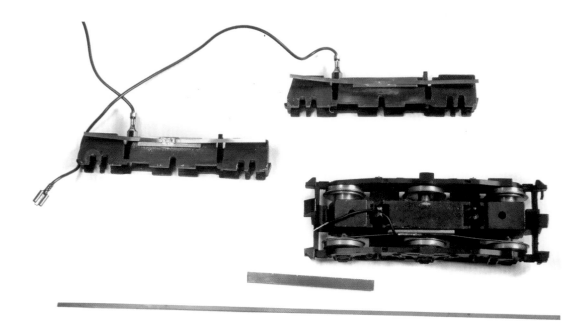

Many older models benefited from additional current collection pickups that could be made up as shown here, using phosphor bronze strip soldered to pieces of PCB copper clad strip.

Slow speed control and delicate train handling require the best performance from a model locomotive, especially from an engine dedicated to shunting and slow speed operation. I probably spend more time working on these to refine their operation than on any others in my collection, especially with regard to current collection pickups.

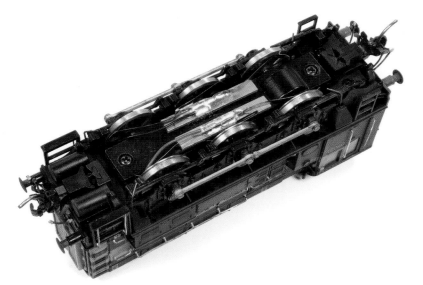

Bachmann Class 08 and Class 09 shunters were originally fitted with radial current collection pickups that made contact with the running surface of the wheel tyre. The result was excess dirt collection, which was cured by fitting more conventional pickups using PCB and phosphor bronze strip. Nickel silver wire could be used instead of phosphor bronze strip.

While on the subject of current pickups, note how the exposed metal glints through the painted plastic detail on this Bachmann model of a Class 411 4-Cep EMU.

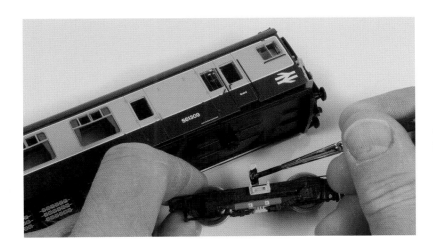

A few seconds' work with black paint soon removes the shine!

REPLACEMENT DRIVE SYSTEMS

Aftermarket drive systems are available to overcome many of the problems with old motor bogies and to upgrade new generation drives with mechanical clutches that create the effects of inertia using mechanical technology rather than the electronic technology available in Digital Command Control decoders. One of the simplest replacement drive system solutions available is a cleverly engineered motor and mounting combination produced by ModelTorque, which replaces the armature and spindle in the Lima drive bogie. It is a very simple conversion to undertake, yet the improvement in operation is quite dramatic. It is described as a project later in this chapter.

ModelTorque also offers its Automatic Torque-control Coupling (ATC) and Sealed Miniature Automatic Transmission (SMAT) technology to modify the performance of a model locomotive to match the effects of loaded trains and the ability of the locomotive to accelerate and decelerate with loads in the same manner as would be experienced when driving a full-size train. ATC is offered as a complete motor and coupling assembly designed to drop straight into a ready-to-run locomotive chassis after the original motor and twin flywheels have been removed. SMAT, on the other hand, is a straightforward replacement for the flywheels fitted to models with motor and flywheel drive mechanisms, using the original motor. SMAT may better suit steam locomotives and diesel shunters where there may be only one flywheel as part of the mechanism, whereas ATC would suit diesel and electric locomotives where there is a frame-mounted motor driving two bogies via twin flywheels and drive shafts.

An original Lima 3-axle drive bogie as fitted to a Class 66 model. Such drives can be upgraded with a ModelTorque motor if better performance is needed, or if the motor is worn out.

PROJECTS

LOCOMOTIVE CURRENT COLLECTION PICKUPS

This project looks at the fitting of additional current collection pickups to one of the first batch of Bachmann Class 66 locomotives to be released. The technique can be adapted to suit a variety of different models and is based on the method of using nickel silver wire and ¼ inch 10BA slotted brass screws.

This method provides a more secure way of mounting pickups than using phosphor bronze strip and copper PCB glued to the locomotive frames, which can come adrift after time. Using a screw for a mounting is less likely to be affected by lubricants than adhesive. Furthermore, nickel silver wire is strong, yet springy enough to provide enough pressure on the rear face of the wheel for efficient current collection.

It takes about an hour to complete the fitting of pickups to both bogies, on both sides, so that the model is capable of collecting current from all of its wheels. You can adapt this technique to suit almost any model, for example fitting extra pickups to a steam locomotive tender or to improve current collection in former Lima models. A factor that has made this improvement even more desirable is that some manufacturers have identified the lack of pickup of current as a cause of TV interference.

The first batch of Class 66 locomotives to be released by Bachmann were fitted with current collection pickups on the inner two axles of each bogie, resulting in less than efficient operation over complex track formations.

It is a simple task to fit new pickups to replace those that have worn out or to supplement what is already there. In most cases it is unnecessary to remove the loco body, as only the bogie or wheel keeper plate should be unclipped.

The usual arrangement of a 6-axle drive locomotive is seen here, with all wheels driven and pickups on the rearmost axles. This is the case with many of Bachmann's earlier releases of this model and others such as the Class 37.

Note the lack of pickups on the forward axle: it's those wheels that need fitting with current collection.

A slotted 10BA brass screw is checked for size to see if it will clear the drive gears.

A 1.5mm diameter hole is drilled through the bogie frame, taking care to catch any plastic debris before it gets clogged in the gears. This task is repeated for both sides of the frame.

Both screws are cut short so they do not touch each other across the bogie frame, causing a short circuit. They easily self-tap into the drilled holes because the plastic frame is relatively soft

A length of 0.45mm nickel silver wire is soldered to the screwhead, using the slot to hold it in place while the soldering iron is applied. A connection with the existing pickup is made simply by soldering one end of the wire to it.

The wheel end of the wire is shaped to work on the rear face of the wheel to collect current.

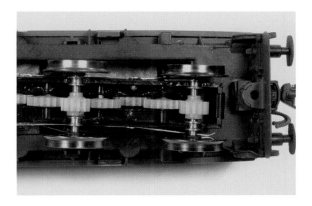

LEFT: A top-down view of the modification showing how the pickups are sprung against the back of the wheels – not too tight, however, or excessive friction will damage the wheel and may make an irritating scraping noise.

BELOW: The bogie frame is clipped back into place and the model tested. Usually a simple modification such as this hugely improves reliability.

REVITALIZING LIMA PANCAKE MOTORS

The obsolete Lima pancake motor and drive has had its day with the demise of Lima. It has been a source of irritation to modellers for some considerable time and consequently its passing will not be mourned. Many of them remain in service on layouts up and down the country, however, and indeed Lima models manufactured for overseas markets are also equipped with them. Not all modellers wish to dispose of their collections in favour of new releases from Hornby, ViTrains, Bachmann and Heljan. Nonetheless, some

drives will be wearing out and performance deteriorating rapidly as a result.

ModelTorque offers an economical and simple to use kit that enables much of the Lima drive to be replaced with a high-fidelity motor and transmission gear and bearing shaft. The kit consists of a motor and mounting plate assembly, together with separate gears to enable an effective connection to the existing Lima gear train.

The conversion is a straightforward project to complete, well within the capabilities of novice modellers and a breeze for the experienced, taking little more than thirty minutes to complete. The result is

A Lima Class 60 needs a motor and drive with enough power to emulate the power of the full-size locomotives. Options include double motoring, such as fitting two drive bogies, or fitting a completely new motor and drive components. This project describes how a Lima motor bogie can be revitalized using a ModelTorque motor replacement product.

To fit a ModelTorque drive replacement unit, the Lima motor is dismantled by releasing the two screws that retain the carbon brushes and armature. Keep the two retaining screws for reuse and discard the rest.

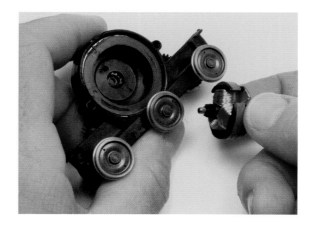

Pull the armature out of the motor housing and dispose of it responsibly.

Insert a flat-bladed screwdriver in between the motor casing and ring magnet. A quick twist will spring the magnet from the housing, which can also be disposed of.

The empty motor housing is ready to accept new parts. Before anything is fitted, check that the remaining final drive gears are free running and that the casing is clean. Fit the gear/bearing assembly into the recess at the back of the motor housing.

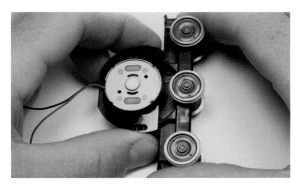

A washer provided in the kit may seem, on first inspection, to be too large to have any real function. It is there to help you press home the drive gear and bearing assembly until it is flush with the motor casing.

The motor and bracket plate, supplied as one assembly, is a direct replacement for the brush holder plate that originally retained the armature and carbon brushes. The right-hand side has a fixed hole designed to take a retaining screw. The left-hand hole is an adjustable slot that can be used to carefully position the bracket plate to ensure that the motor pinion meshes correctly with the gears within the motor housing. Adjust the position of the bracket with the adjustable slot before tightening the screws. The idea is to achieve smooth running by feel, since it is impossible to have sight of the gears without drilling a view hole through the motor casing.

ABOVE: Secure the right-hand side (fixed) screw first, leaving just enough slack to enable adjustment of the motor and plate. A nylon washer is provided in the kit. Note that the original screws are used.

RIGHT: The completed unit assembled, tested and installed in a Lima Class 60 locomotive. A small amount of the plastic cab insert must be pared away to prevent it fouling the new motor casing.

a drive that is more controllable and with a slightly higher top speed. It can be fitted to both 2- and 3-axle drive bogies and tender drive motors in older Lima steam locomotive models. The sequence of images on pages 116–117 demonstrates the conversion process. No special tools are required to complete the conversion: all you will need is a screwdriver and a soldering iron.

MOTOR-DRIVEN COOLING FANS FOR A HORNBY CLASS 56

Full-size diesel electric locomotives need effective regulation of engine temperature to ensure efficient operation. This is controlled through a bank of radiators and a mechanism to draw air through the radiators – in other words, a fan or two. Rarely are the fan mechanisms dependent on engine speed and direction of the locomotive. On modern diesel locomotives, it is more likely controlled with a thermostat that monitors temperature levels and controls the cooling system accordingly, keeping the engine at optimum temperature. It is not unusual to see locomotives running at speed but without the fans rotating or rotating only slowly. At the same time, stationary locomotives may be running hot and the fans will be doing their job of drawing cool air through the radiators.

New-generation models of diesel electric locomotives produced by Hornby are, with the exception of the Class 60, fitted with a working cooling fan mechanism, taking advantage of the etched metal roof grilles that are part of the higher level of detail on models produced today. The simplest and most cost-effective way to drive the fan was via a linkage to the locomotive drive. Hornby chose a simple rubber band drive to form that linkage, but the downside of this feature is that it is dependent on the direction of travel and the operating speed of the model, causing the fans to rotate and speed up or slow down as the locomotive's speed is changed, which is not prototypical. To be fair, it's not a bad working compromise to suit an off-the-shelf model and, more importantly, the fan mechanism itself is well designed, leaving it open to enhancement with an electric motor, of course.

The objective of this project is to enjoy independent control of the cooling fans in a Hornby Class 56 regardless of the direction of travel of the locomotive and its speed by motorizing the fans and controlling them with a decoder. The same approach could be adapted to suit almost any Hornby diesel model equipped with fans. The fan drive mechanism is also available as a spare through Hornby stockists, so it could be adapted to suit other brands of model.

Why DCC controlled?

One of the major benefits of DCC is the ability to control various features of a model independently of track power. Modellers will be familiar with using function outputs for realistic control of running lights and the motor output for a realistic driving experience that is not dependent on controlling the power in the track. The same principle can be applied to cooling fans and DCC is the only practical way of controlling the motor used to drive the cooling fans, enabling the speed and direction to be carefully set independently of anything else. Some modellers may argue that battery power and reed switches could be incorporated instead of using DCC should the model be used on an analogue layout. However, experience shows that the additional space required for batteries and their short life expectancy makes it a cumbersome alternative to DCC.

Thinking about how to power the motor, I decided against using one of the function outputs from the main locomotive decoder for several reasons: firstly, I wanted to be able to control the speed and direction of the fans; secondly, the rated power output of any particular function output is unlikely to be more than 100mA, which could be exceeded by the motor. I chose to use the motor output of a second decoder to power the fans (referred to as a 'secondary decoder' throughout this project so it can be differentiated from the main drive decoder). Before the decoder was installed, it was programmed with its own address independent of the drive decoder so that control of the fans would not be affected by instructions sent to the main drive decoder.

Tools and materials

The following tools and materials were to hand on the workbench to complete the project:

- General modeller's hand tools including jewellers' screwdrivers, modelling knife and blades.
- Soldering iron and electrical solder.
- A Hornby decoder to be used as a secondary decoder.
- Scraps of 40 thou styrene.
- Mashima 10 × 20mm flat can motor (Mashima 1020).
- Medium viscosity superglue.
- Mini drill and carborundum cutting disc.

Workbench time

It took approximately two hours to dismantle the relevant part of the Class 56, remove the fan mechanism, modify it, reinstall and connect the secondary decoder. No modification to the bodyshell, either internally or externally, was necessary to make it all work.

Four retaining screws secure the body to the chassis. Once released, the body slides straight off and can be placed to one side. Examine the fan mechanism carefully, locate and remove the rubber drive band by snipping it with scissors and pulling it clear

with tweezers. The fan mechanism is removed and the cover taken off the drive shaft so that it can be removed together with its bearings.

On the end of the drive shaft is located a small piece of silicone tube, which is the part that makes contact with the fan mechanism itself. It acts like a tyre, providing grip to ensure that the fans rotate without the need for an additional set of gears. Remove and retain the silicone tubing.

The Mashima 1020 motor is modified to fit in the space vacated by the drive shaft. My choice of Mashima motor has a drive shaft with 10mm clear at each end. The one at the end with the electrical terminals should be cut as short as possible; the opposite one should be cut to the length of the piece of silicone tube, approximately 4mm in length.

The plastic frame that holds the drive shaft and bearings is modified to accept the motor by cutting away most of the plastic to leave a smooth floor. The motor, due to its size, is installed at a slight angle so that the silicone tube 'tyre' acts upon the fan drive, as seen in the photographs. The motor can be secured to the frame using small pieces of styrene card to support it and a drop of superglue.

The mechanism, together with the smooth-running Mashima motor, is tested out of the model using

Hornby released its brand-new model of the Class 56 in 2007. In common with others of its new-generation models of diesel electric locomotives, all three versions were equipped with opening cab doors, running lights and rotating cooling fans. The one exception was the Class 60, which has no cooling fans visible to the outside.

an ordinary power pack to see that all is rotating smoothly. Sometimes small pieces of plastic from the modifications to the frame get into somewhere they shouldn't, and these should be removed prior to testing. Once satisfied with performance, the assembly can be refitted to the model.

Installing the decoder is straightforward. The red and black harness wires are soldered to the track power supply terminals on the model's circuit board, bypassing the NEM DCC interface socket. The orange and grey wires are connected to the motor terminals. It's as simple as that. The decoder's unique address is chosen and the speed of the fans set to suit the operating situation. The setting could be left like that on a permanent basis or changed while the locomotive is in operation by selecting the secondary decoder address from a stack in the throttle.

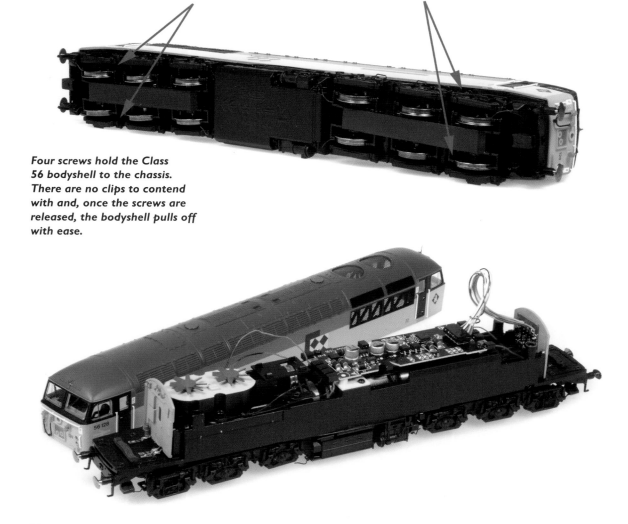

Four screws hold the Class 56 bodyshell to the chassis. There are no clips to contend with and, once the screws are released, the bodyshell pulls off with ease.

The mechanism in the Class 56 model is sophisticated and features a belt-driven fan mechanism, which can be seen nearest the camera. It is this mechanism that makes this project possible using a motor and decoder.

Four screws hold the fan
mechanism in place. The drive
belt is removed first and then
the whole assembly unscrewed
and transferred to the
workbench.

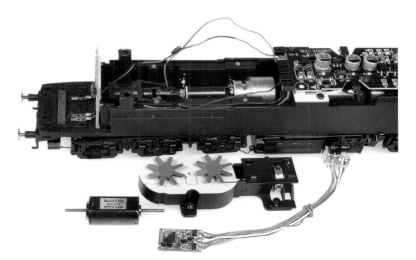

The component parts for the
project include a new Hornby
four-function decoder, chosen
for its low cost but smooth
performance, and a Mashima
10 × 20mm flat can motor.

The secondary decoder is
programmed with a number
different from that allocated to
the locomotive decoder before
installation. The red and black
wires are soldered directly to
the track supply terminals on
the circuit board (A) and (B).
The orange and grey wires are
connected to the Mashima
motor once it is installed (C).
The unused function wires are
bundled together so they do not
get in the way (D).

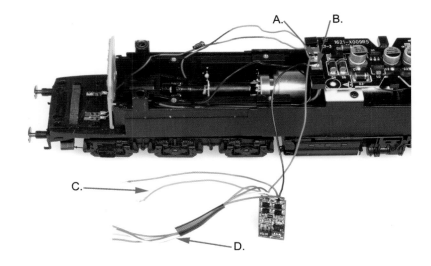

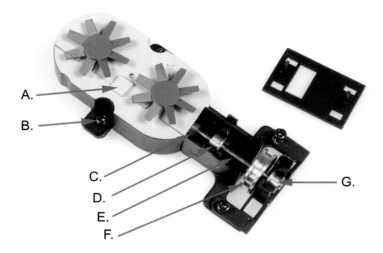

A.

B.

C.

D.

E.

F.

G.

The fan drive mechanism is extensively modified to accommodate the motor. Note the location of the various components including fixing screws (B): the method of fixing this to the chassis should not be changed. Access to the interior of the drive mechanism is by unclipping the side of the fan housing (A). The end of the drive shaft (E) has a silicone sleeve that works on the fan mechanism to enable them to rotate (C). Bearings are provided at (D) and (G), while the belt drive wheel can be seen at (F).

The fan drive mechanism is dismantled like this. The drive shaft and bearings are discarded except for the silicone sleeve, which is reused.

Some experimentation with regard to the fit of the motor was necessary at first to see how much modification had to be done to the plastic moulding.

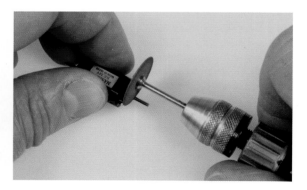

So that the motor would fit between the fan housing and the circuit board, the drive shafts were shortened using a cutting disc.

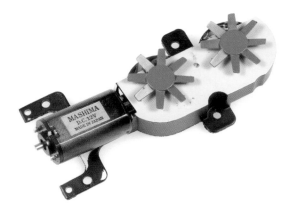

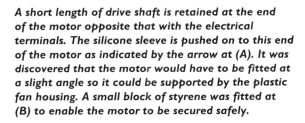

A short length of drive shaft is retained at the end of the motor opposite that with the electrical terminals. The silicone sleeve is pushed on to this end of the motor as indicated by the arrow at (A). It was discovered that the motor would have to be fitted at a slight angle so it could be supported by the plastic fan housing. A small block of styrene was fitted at (B) to enable the motor to be secured safely.

The modified fan mechanism completed and ready to be installed in the locomotive.

A side view of the completed project. Note how the inclined motor does not extend much above the height of the roof fans, which means the bodyshell will fit back on the chassis without the motor touching it and causing unwanted vibration.

You wouldn't guess that these fans are driven by a small precision motor, such is the neat appearance of the drive mechanism fitted to the Hornby Class 56.

RE-MOTORING A HORNBY PACER

Hornby released a model of the Class 142 some years ago and has provided versions of the unit in various liveries. The bodyshell represents the Class in its 'as built' condition with folding doors and without radio telephone pods. It has all the hallmarks of the older generation of Hornby models including its Achilles heel: the drive. In reality, the drive (or drives, because there are two of them, one in each car) fitted to the Hornby model is pretty accurate: it could not pull the skin off a rice pudding and it is noisy, unreliable and difficult to control. Not too dissimilar to the real thing!

This is to the regret of some modellers because the Class 142 model is reasonably accurate and would form an ideal base-line for reworking into something very reasonable indeed. The basic design of the underframe and the drive makes a reliability upgrade something of a challenge. Ideally one car should be powered with both axles driven rather than the current arrangement of one drive in each vehicle powering just one axle. The wiring in each vehicle of the two-car set is not linked across the coupling, which means that one vehicle can stall while the other is still grinding away! Some modellers have overcome the problem of poor current collection by installing jumper wires between the vehicles, thus extending the practical collection of electrical current over both vehicles for both drives.

No matter what you do to the original arrangement, though, you cannot make a silk purse out of this particular 'nodding donkey's' ear.

A company called Branchlines Models developed a replacement drive and compensation unit kit for the Hornby 'Pacer' in 2000. It is designed to replace the noisy unreliable drive with something a little more refined. This makes a surprisingly simple project, requiring basic soldering skills and the normal tools found in the average modeller's toolbox. It is possible to complete the conversion from donkey's ear to something approaching a coarse cotton money bag, if not a silk purse, in an afternoon of careful work. Be advised that the conversion kit does not include the parts to power both vehicles, only one five-pole motor is supplied, together with a 38:1 gear set. Although it is described as a chassis kit, the only parts provided are those to replace the drive assemblies, so you will end up with just a single powered axle out of four ... unless you buy an additional motor, 38:1 gear set and flywheel.

Nonetheless, the kit is of good quality with accurately etched trailing and powered sub-chassis frames together with the inclusion of a quality, if small, Mashima five-pole motor, Ultrascale gears and a good selection of accurately turned bearings and bushes. Four pages of comprehensive instructions are included. Wheel sets are available in all of

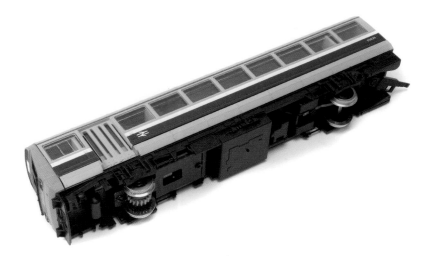

The 'Pacer' model produced by Hornby never really set the hobby alight when it was introduced some years ago. Today it looks decidedly dated compared to the refined toolings now being offered by the company. It sits in that era where it was routine to spend money and time making refinements and improvements to mediocre ready-to-run models. How times have changed!

the popular gauges and are usually the same type of wheel as used in Black Beetle motor bogies.

Starting with a complete model, remove the original drive and trailing axle assembly from each vehicle. Those items may be discarded, never to be used again. One vehicle should be chosen to be the trailing car and this is used for dry run assembly to ensure that everything fits together comfortably. Start by assembling one trailing axle rocking assembly, folding the etched frames with the half-etched lines on the inside of the fold. A fillet of solder is run along the inside corner of each fold for strength. The rocking unit is fitted with $1/8$ inch diameter axle bearings, which are then reduced to 2mm diameter using reducing bushes so they will accept the wheels supplied in the kit. The assembly is then test fitted to the model before being dismantled again and the etched frames primed and painted 'off the model'.

Next turn attention to the second frame, which is designed to hold the motor and gears. Because only one vehicle is powered, one frame is assembled as a second trailing axle assembly for the trailing car. Again, this is simply folded up and reinforced with solder. The same arrangement with the axle bushes is applied, with 2mm reducing bushes fitted to $1/8$ inch diameter bushes before the wheel set is fitted.

The trailing car is completed by the fitting of the completed axle assemblies. Care is taken to ensure that the live wheel on each wheel set is positioned on the same side of the underframe for current collection or a short circuit results. Each axle assembly is linked by a connecting wire that terminates at the gangway end ready for connection to the powered car.

The trailing axle assembly on the powered car is made up in the same manner as that used on the trailing car. However, there is a little more work to do on the powered sub-chassis frame. The motor and flywheel are fixed to the second soldered and painted frame using two small screws supplied in the kit. The worm gear is a push fit onto the motor shaft. The wheel set is fitted with the reducing bushes and the final drive gear, which is secured with a tiny drop of Loctite 603, taking care not to run the glue into the axle bushes. The assembly can be electrically tested once you are confident that the glue has hardened completely.

Once satisfied with the drive sub-chassis, it may be test-fitted to the underframe and, if that is satisfactory, secured with two self-tapping screws. One motor terminal may be connected directly to the chassis frame, collecting current from the live wheel via the axle. The other motor terminal may be linked directly to the gangway end of the model for connection with the trailing vehicle. When completing the assembly of the driven car, ensure that the live

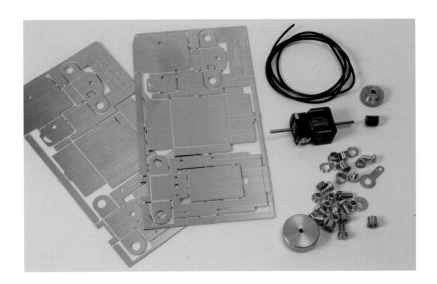

The Branchlines Models replacement drive kit for the Hornby 'Pacer' is based on traditional methods and materials with an etched nickel silver sub-chassis and the usual collection of gears, bearings and a flywheel making up the majority of the components.

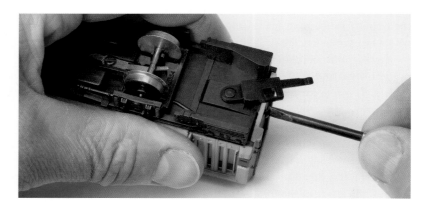

A single screw located at the gangway end of each vehicle secures the body to the underframe.

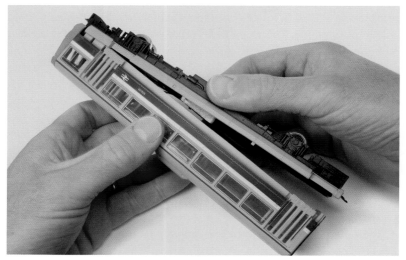

The whole body assembly together with the interior moulding simply pulls away from the underframe.

wheels of both axles are on the same side of the underframe, but opposite to that of the trailing car when they are coupled back to back. This will ensure that you will have current collection from both rails. Additional pickups could be added to the insulated wheel of each wheel set for eight-wheel pickup throughout the unit.

After lubricating the axle bushes and the gears, the model should be tested on a section of level track. In this project it became clear that additional ballast would be required to improve the adhesion of the model: I very much doubt that the model would be able to tackle even the slightest incline unless the trailing vehicle is also equipped with motor and gears.

Two screws secure the drive assembly to the underframe: one is located on the inside of the underframe.

The other screw is located on the underside of the underframe. Once both screws are released, the drive unit drops out from the bottom of the underframe. Also remove and discard the inner end axle assembly.

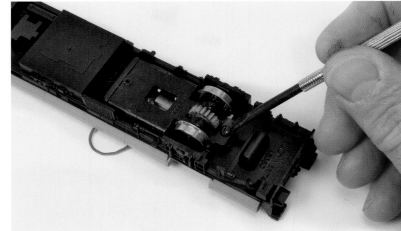

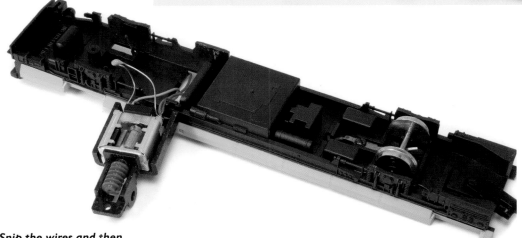

ABOVE: **Snip the wires and then discard the old drive assembly. Note the crude current collection pickups that are designed to work on the tyre of the wheels. The pickups should also be removed and discarded because current collection on the replacement drive works through the 'live' wheel and axle on each wheel set.**

RIGHT: **Some modifications are made to the plastic underframe to ensure that the new drive assembly will drop neatly into place. Some plastic is removed from the powered end of the underframe to make room for the flywheel in the powered car.**

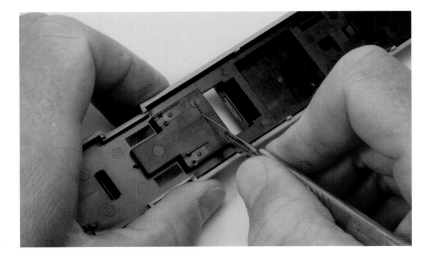

Compensation based on the simple 'three point compensation' method is designed into the kit and the trailing axle assembly is designed with a compensation rocking unit. The trailing axle assembly and baseplate simply fold up as shown in this image. A spare $^1/_8$ inch diameter axle is used to assist with fitting the axle bearings. Reducing bushes are included in the kit to allow the use of the wheel sets supplied with the kit, which have 2mm diameter axles.

Both completed trailing axle assemblies are shown with Black Beetle wheels to EM gauge fitted to the rocking unit. This is a test assembly to check that the etched components are assembled true and square. Furthermore, test-fitting to the underframe reveals where adjustments may be necessary for smooth running. The assemblies are taken apart again for painting 'off the model'.

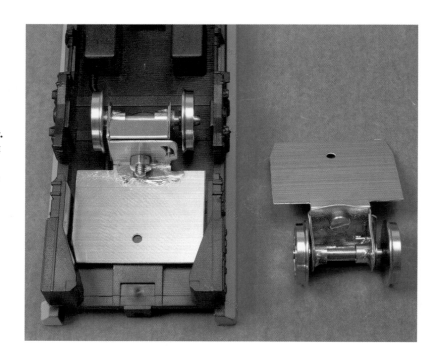

The etched frame drops neatly into the recess vacated by the original drive sub-chassis. Note the location of the two etched screw holes in the frame and mark the exact position on the underframe. Remove the etched frame and drill two pilot holes into the underframe using a 2mm diameter drill.

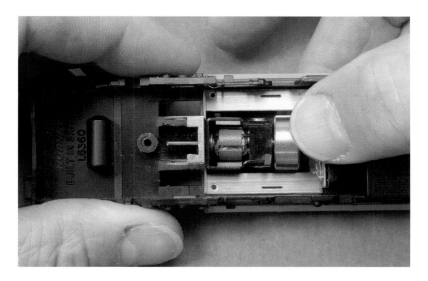

On the powered car, it is possible to carry out a dry run fit of the motor and flywheel to ensure that sufficient plastic has been removed from the underframe to clear the flywheel.

The frame is painted before final assembly of the motor and gears. The motor is fitted to the frame with the two mounting screws once the paint has fully dried.

The wheel set and gears are assembled to the powered drive unit.

A completed drive unit ready for installation. The pinpoint axles are filed back, although this is not absolutely necessary for good running.

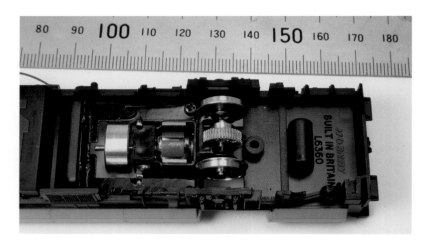

Two screw holes etched in the frame are designed to accept self-tapping screws supplied with the kit. The screws should self-tap into the pilot holes drilled into the plastic underframe and will secure the drive unit to the plastic underframe.

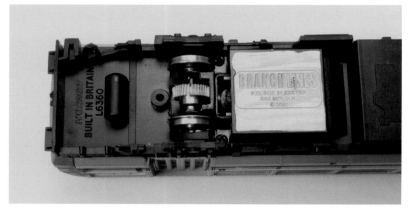

An etched box conceals the drive assembly and is a fair representation of the underframe fuel tank. A similar arrangement is provided for the trailing car.

The backbone of local train services has been provided since 1985 by railbuses such as the Class 142 'Pacer'. Some long-distance trains operated over lightly used lines, such as the Carlisle–Middlesbrough via Newcastle upon Tyne services, also employ Class 142s. 'Pacer' No. 142024 stands in a bay platform at Carlisle prior to its departure for Middlesbrough. The livery is unbranded Arriva blue and cream, an attractive scheme. As for the ride over the Tyne Valley Line, it would probably be on the bouncy side. Carlisle, 1 June 2005.

DEALING WITH UNSPRUNG MIDDLE AXLES

There are a number of 6-axle diesel electric locomotive models, notably by Heljan and ViTrains, that do not have a powered middle axle on both bogies. It is also unusual for those axles to be sprung and, with no gear train to hold them in place, they can flop around without any real guidance to keep them on the rails. In effect, they do not take any load from the locomotive at all.

This simple project demonstrates how springing can be introduced to keep such unpowered axles on the rails. Placing a light sprung load on the axle improves road holding and locomotive performance. The materials are basically the same as when fitting additional current pickups, except the spring is not connected to any part of the model's wiring. A Heljan Class 47 is used to demonstrate this technique, which employs 0.45mm diameter nickel silver wire as a spring and four ¼in 10BA countersunk screws as a convenient mount. You will need a 1.5mm drill and pin vice to complete the project.

The locomotive does not have to be dismantled to complete the project, only the bogie side frames and baseplate removed to gain access to the wheels. It takes less than 30 minutes to fit four springs, two to each bogie.

The Heljan Class 47 with bogie side frames removed, exposing the phosphor bronze pickups. The middle axle has no pickups, so this model could be improved by fitting some in the same manner as the Class 66 described earlier.

Note how the middle axle simply has no role to play in either collecting power from the rails or guiding the bogie through track formations. It simply flops about.

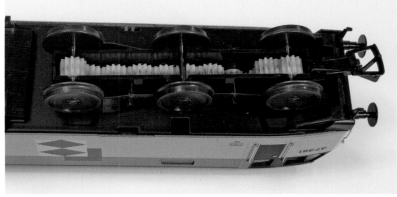

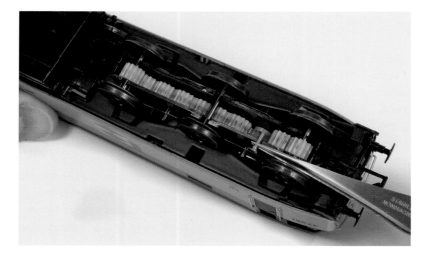

The springs will be mounted on ¼in 10BA screws. A suitable position to fit them is determined so they do not foul the gears.

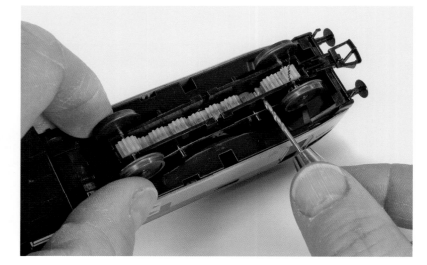

1.5mm diameter holes are drilled through the bogie frame.

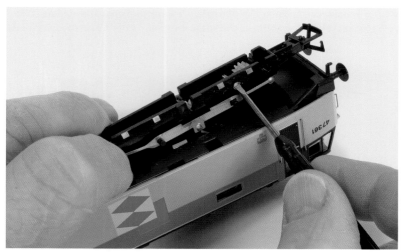

The 10BA screws (shortened) self-tap into the soft plastic.

A length of nickel silver wire is soldered to the screw head to create a spring.

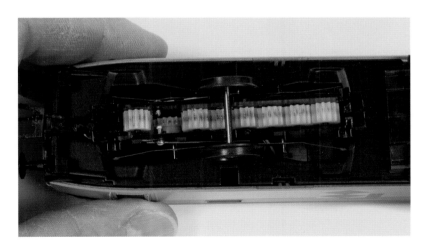

One spring is fitted to each side of the bogie to even out the downward force on the axle.

Two of the baseplate retaining clips interfere with the working of the springs. They are snipped away without worrying about fixing: there are more than enough left to do the job.

The baseplate is reinstated. Note that the clips removed from the baseplate do not prevent it from fitting securely to the model.

While the bogie frames are sitting on the workbench, paint the very prominent pickups with grey paint to reduce their impact on the model's appearance.

The project is complete and the appearance is much improved by painting the exposed metal components before replacing the bogie side frames.

CONCLUSION

With fine tuning of the model complete, either to improve reliability or to replace worn drive components, the next stage of preparing a model for use on the layout can be considered. The process of simple detailing and customization, work that does not cost the earth in terms of time and materials, is described in the next chapter. In effect, it covers simple techniques for transforming a model from a mass-produced, shiny, out-of-the-box product into something that looks like 100 tons plus of grimy, oily, hard-worked machinery, with minimal effort. At the same time, if a change of identity is needed, that is possible too, and in all likelihood without repainting the whole model.

A Heljan Class 47 fitted with springing to the middle axles of each bogie, which improves the ability of the locomotive to stay on the rails through complex trackwork. The once unsprung wheels had a tendency to derail and ride over check and switch rails rather than riding through the flange ways.

CHAPTER FIVE

SIMPLE ENHANCEMENTS

The paint finishes on models produced by the mainstream manufacturers today rarely need any attention other than refinement and weathering thanks to good research and accurate application. The Heljan Class 33 featured here was renumbered and fitted out with buffer beam details before being weathered, but little else was done to customize it. Nonetheless, it is unique to my collection thanks to that additional work.

INTRODUCTION

One of the advantages of the new genre of models, with their perfect paint finishes and quality detail, is that many projects of old required to beat into submission a lump of plastic that approximates to some locomotive or other are no longer littering our workbenches. Nonetheless, there is always room to take an existing ready-to-run model and enhance it with simple detailing and weathering, even if all you do is fit the add-on detailing pack supplied in the box (*see* Chapter 2).

One problem with all these lovely new models we are able to buy today, however, is the likelihood of the appearance of identical-looking models on exhibition and private layouts. There are two reasons why this may occur. Firstly, the quality of paint finish offered with new models is far superior to anything that the majority of us can achieve with an airbrush, and few modellers will be prepared to strip and over-paint it. Secondly, it is a shame to completely obliterate a factory-applied livery as good and as accurate as those found on contemporary standard

models issued by Hornby, Bachmann and ViTrains. After all, we have paid for that paint finish as part of the overall price for the model, both in terms of research and its application. While repainting a model is the only way to obtain a livery that is not available on some model at any given time, it is worth adding up the total cost of a repaint job, which may include transfers, nameplates, paint colours, depot plaques and lining, together with the necessary consumables such as masking tape and paint thinner. Yes, repainting something which takes you 85 per cent of the way to your objective, straight from the box, does not always make sense.

With those thoughts in mind, this chapter looks at another area of model refinement that brings great results without you having to spend a packet on modelling materials. It is a form of pragmatic modelling that saves time and money, and releases time for the modeller to build rolling stock, layouts, scenery and structures. In this chapter I present various methods for simple customizing of ready-to-run locomotive models without having to fully repaint them. In the process, something very unique is the result.

REFERENCE MATERIAL

When following the principles of prototype modelling, it is useful to have some reference photographs to hand. The internet has gone a long way to supply material that can be used to verify the details and livery elements for a particular locomotive project. Nonetheless, I still find that books are the best source of reference material, followed by my own personal collection of photographs. The latter has grown over the years as I photograph railway equipment I feel may make an excellent modelling subject in the future.

A Class 08 shunter model acquired for my Dudley Heath Yard layout is a good example. Seeking suitable shunters to work the layout, I found, in my photographic collection, an image of 08 456 working at Bescot Yard, which was invaluable for verifying specific details and how the locomotive had weathered over the years. A one-time long-term West Midlands resident, 08 456 was perfect for my layout.

I used a suitable Hornby model with the correct class-specific details as a basis for the project and simply resprayed the main body colour, nothing else. I retained the yellow and black stripes on the ends of the bodyshell because they were the hardest part to paint and finish. By the time I had weathered it and added the details supplied with the model, it was unrecognizable from the original, as the project described below illustrates. Another model that was renumbered but not repainted for my collection was a Hornby Class 60 in EWS colours, which evolved into a completely different beast when simply treated to lining and numbering transfers together with weathering. The main objective of all such projects that pass across my workbench is to choose a prototype that matches the model closely so the livery colours could be retained, saving a great deal of money and time. Once a suitable reference picture is found, work can proceed quickly.

While it is tempting to leave a special edition model in the box, why not give it a make-over and put it to use on the layout? After all, models like this limited edition Class 57 by Bachmann are made to run! Simple enhancement techniques have been applied to this model: weathering to wheels, underframe and roof is about the only paint applied to it.

The popular former Lima Class 121 'Pressed Steel' DMU single car can be rebuilt, with minimal painting, into a Gloucester Class 122 single-car unit. Many ready-to-run models offer opportunities for simple enhancement and detailing to create something a little different.

The result of rebuilding the Class 122 model. Apart from the roof and cab fronts, the original livery was retained, even though the conversion work was relatively involved.

The resulting Class 122 model is seen in the layout environment where its Hornby origins are not obvious.

Colas Rail 47 739 is one of the projects in this chapter that demonstrate simple refinement techniques that can be applied to a ready-to-run model. The real locomotive was displayed at Carlisle Kingmoor in July 2009, showing useful details from the No. 2 end for the modeller. Note the use of elliptical buffers and the fitting of a multiple working socket to the headcode panel. The multiple working equipment fitted to the front of 47 739 by BR Rail Express Systems in the early 1990s was removed when overhauled at Eastleigh.

Looking the part on the layout following simple detailing and weathering. One cannot tell if the paint is original, and at this distance, it does not matter.

Another example of a minimalist project is Class 08 shunter, No. 08 567, a locomotive that attracted my attention because of its bleached weathering and interesting detail. It was photographed in BR blue livery at Bescot in 2002, and this useful reference photograph shows interesting features to model, including buffers that differ from one end to the other, swing buckeye couplings, a sealed-up cab roof vent and up-to-date electrification warning notices.

THE MINIMALIST APPROACH

I have found myself increasingly taking this approach to locomotive modelling primarily because of the time it saves and the satisfaction of a quick result. Models are quickly placed in service and have a unique appearance because, no matter how uniform the manufacturing and finishing of the model straight from the factory, no two modellers will achieve exactly the same result after applying minimalist detailing.

The most common form of customization is simply to renumber the model based on information gleaned from record books and photographs. Both waterslide and Pressfix transfers can be used very effectively to completely change the identity of both steam locomotives and diesel electrics. The process is as simple as removing the printed number from the model without damaging the underlying paint finish and applying the new number. Sometimes a new nameplate is also required, so check to see if your chosen 'namer' can be recreated. The process for simple renumbering is as follows:

- Carefully remove the unwanted number by using a gentle solvent that will soften the printing. Suitable solvents include IPA and Microscale Decal Sol transfer setting solution. Apply a small drop to the treatment area and leave for a couple of minutes before gently

rubbing away with a cotton bud – don't rub too hard or you will remove paint too.
- The top layer of varnish applied to the model will be removed in the process, usually revealing a gloss painted finish. Don't be alarmed by that development, it's to your advantage with this process.
- Apply the new numbers following the instructions supplied with the transfer pack. Any underlying gloss finish will provide the ideal surface to hide any carrier film. Leave to dry overnight.
- Spot spray matt varnish to the treated area to remove the glossy finish and blend in your work before moving onto any weathering effects.

MINIMALIST CUSTOMIZATION

The following techniques can be applied to almost any model to customize it for use on your layout. The idea is to remove the typical 'factory finish' and make the model look like a miniature version of something built of steel and weighing many tons!

- Look for paint shadows around raised detail, behind the buffer beams and other similar areas that do little for the model's appearance. Touch them in with the appropriate body colour. The insides of window frames particularly benefit from a thin application of black

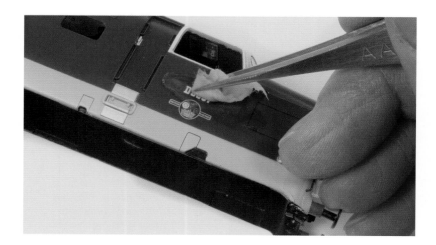

When the livery finish is too good to repaint, it is simple to erase running numbers and other printed detail using a solvent such as IPA and a piece of kitchen roll tissue, as demonstrated here. Discolouring from the dissolved print is easily cleaned off afterwards.

paint, especially when the model is painted in a light-coloured livery or has a bodyshell moulded from a light-coloured plastic.

- Paint the wheel faces on diesel electrics and be prepared to do the same to steam locomotive wheel rims if there is no blackened metal finish. This makes such a difference to the appearance of the model.
- Weather the coupling rods and valve gear of steam locomotives. Coal dust and water staining soon takes its toll on hard-worked locomotives.
- Look for phosphor bronze pickups peeking from behind locomotive frames and bogie side frames. Touch in with dark grey to disguise this unwanted gleam of metal.
- Weather the underframes and wheels using reference photographs for guidance. Avoid using black for soot and diesel exhaust carbon staining: dark grey is much better.
- Add cab detail, including a driver and second man.
- Fit etched nameplates over painted ones.
- Add class-specific details to the buffer beam, including brake pipes and jumper cables. Ensure they are weathered with the rest of the model.

Ensure that all the work you do is consistently applied. This will help to disguise any plastic appearance the model may have resulting from corner cutting by the manufacturer. For example, some separately applied details may be unpainted, with the manufacturer relying on the base colour of the plastic to achieve the desired result.

PROJECTS

RENUMBER BUT NO REPAINTING

A special commission for a client resulted in my playing around with Hornby 'West Country' (Southern Region) and 'Castle' Class (Western Region) steam locomotives in a renumbering and renaming project to suit his layout aspirations. This uses 'prototype freelancing', a concept common in North America but rarely seen in the UK. The models were not repainted, but simply renumbered. In both cases they were also fitted with new nameplates, some of them bearing freelanced names and numbers outside the full-size steam locomotive's number sequence. In doing so, the modeller has created a unique fleet in a believable manner by adding some freelancing to prototype-based models in a subtle way. I am willing to wager that some enthusiasts won't even notice the fictitious nature of the names and numbers.

This project brings into focus an increasingly common query: how to remove the printed numbers from contemporary standard models so that identities can be changed without the trouble and cost of repainting the model. It's a scary thing for a novice to tackle given that the typical price of a large steam locomotive in OO gauge is between £70 and £110. There is potential for a messy disaster if the wrong materials and techniques are used. However, given the quality of contemporary standard models, this is a technique that should be in every modeller's armoury. You only have to take a look at the printed lining on the Hornby 'West Country' locomotives to wonder if that is something done as neatly with a lining pen or transfers. This project demonstrates how renumbering of ready-to-run steam locomotives can be undertaken. In the case of locomotives of the GWR and Western Region of BR, most had cast number plates that are available as etched plates, making the process straightforward.

The technique

I started work on the Southern Region locomotives by placing a small puddle of Microscale Micro Sol on the numerals, dealing with one side of the locomotive at a time. IPA would work just as well for this task. The solvent was left for about ten minutes to allow it to get to work. A cotton bud was gently rubbed across the numerals to remove them. When I did this for the first time I noticed that the factory-applied varnish was also stripped away to reveal a glossy paint finish ideal for the safe application of new transfers, chosen from the HMRS Pressfix range in this case. One thing you will notice when you try this technique for the first time is that the surface of the paint appears to become cloudy. Traces of the dissolved print will settle on the surface of the model as the Micro Sol dries out. Don't worry about it because it is easily removed with a soft cloth and more Micro Sol. The real challenge is to keep the rubbing action within the confines of the numerals so that other painted or printed detail is not affected.

The transfers were applied next, using photographs of the full-size locomotives as reference to see precisely where to place each numeral. Once finished, the models were left to one side for about twenty-four hours to allow the transfers to set. Masking tape was applied around the treated area and along cab corners, to prevent an obvious paint edge, and a thin coat of matt varnish sprayed over it to seal the transfers in place. The final job involving transfers was to apply new smoke box numbers, which were taken from a waterslide transfer sheet produced by a Scottish transfer producer called Modelmaster. It's very easy to forget about smoke box numbers.

Nameplates, number plates and crests

The pair of Hornby 'Castle' Class engines were renumbered and renamed with etched nameplates and number plates supplied by 247 Developments. Both models have printed nameplates and number plates, making this task quite straightforward. Starting with the cab side number plates, the original printed number plate was gently pared away with a scalpel blade. Printed nameplates were rubbed away with a fibreglass pencil to leave a textured surface that would assist the bonding of the new plates, which were applied with matt varnish. The final task was to attach the smoke box number plate over the printed version. Roughen the rear surface of each plate to provide a key for the varnish. Undertake each part of the job slowly and carefully to avoid getting excess glue onto the model. Renumbering and renaming took only an hour to complete for each locomotive.

I could not apply the same approach to the 'West Country' Class locomotives, the renaming of which involved much more work. Hornby supply these models with separate nameplates and crests that are particularly good – indeed it seems a shame to discard them! The crests are fitted to slots in the side of the streamlining on 'West Country' Class locomotives and are easily removed with tweezers. Unfortunately the nameplates are both clipped and glued into place. No matter how careful I was, traces of the glue remained on the surface of the model.

Two Hornby GWR/BR(W) 'Castle' Class locomotives were renamed and renumbered using etched plates from 247 Developments in this renumbering project.

The GWR/BR(W) 'Castle' Class locomotives have printed nameplate and number plate detail that is easily removed, making the renumbering project simple to do.

Making up the crests using the etchings supplied by 247 Developments to the standard of Hornby's printed plates was quite challenging. The backing for each crest was removed first and traces of the etched cab filed away. Taking the printed herald, I held it up to a window, using the light to see the exact position of the herald so I could carefully pencil in a faint cross on the reverse, with the intersecting lines in the dead centre of the herald to act as a guide for the correct positioning of the crest packing plate, which was glued into place. Excess paper was trimmed away with a sharp scalpel using the crest backing plate as a template. The crest surround was removed from the fret and applied on top of the printed herald. The assembly was then fitted to the model with a tiny spot of superglue.

The nameplates were pinged off the side of the model by inserting the tip of a scalpel blade underneath and twisting gently to release the bond. The same scalpel blade was then used to clean away excess glue that would otherwise prevent the new nameplates from sitting flat on the side of the model. Each nameplate was applied with a tiny spot of matt varnish. The last task involved the application of the tiny crests that bear the legend: West Country Class.

The finished result

I was pleasantly surprised at achieving a reasonably seamless result with the transfers and varnish. This technique is fiddly but saves a great deal of time in avoiding a repaint and revarnish of the model. It is a good way of customizing a model while retaining the quality finishes now being applied by mainstream manufacturers. If desired, subtle weathering can be applied to complete the appearance of an in-service and hard-working steam locomotive.

Nameplates for 'Tempest', which will become No. 5094, are shown in this picture. The etched plate set from 247 Developments includes side number plates and a smoke box number plate. Such plates add something special to a ready-to-run model.

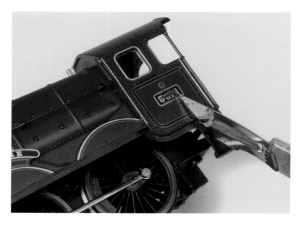

The cab side number plate is removed with the tip of a sharp scalpel blade to leave a roughened surface that acts as a key for the matt varnish used to apply the new number plates.

An alternative way to remove printed detail is to use a fibreglass pencil, which also provides a roughened surface for adhesive such as matt varnish.

No livery paint was harmed in the renaming and renumbering of this locomotive and much time was saved in the process. Weathering can be applied for added character, but that is outside the scope of this project.

The Hornby 'rebuilt' West Country locomotive is particularly attractive and features a great deal of fine detail. It was renumbered as No. 34112 '609 Squadron', a freelanced name and number to suit a prototype freelanced fleet of locomotives.

Assembling the individual crests is a precise job. They are supplied in three parts: the printed herald is glued to the backing piece using pencil lines to obtain the correct alignment, and each crest is finished with an etched frame.

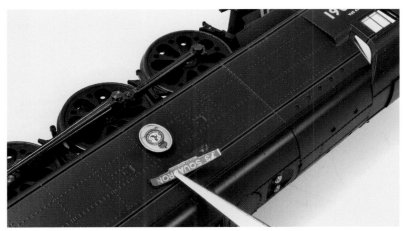

Hornby glues the nameplates on its West Countries. The excess should be removed so the new nameplates will sit flat.

This is where the fun begins! Each crest is made up of the backing piece, the printed herald and the frame. However, although this is a fiddly job the end result is well worth it. The old crest is shown in the foreground.

A new name means a new locomotive number too. The old one is removed with Microscale Micro Sol, which is applied to the area to be treated and left for 10 minutes before gentle rubbing with a cotton bud.

The print soon dissolves away. Note that the surface of the treated area soon appears to become dirty with residue. That is easily removed by rubbing gently with Micro Sol and a soft cloth.

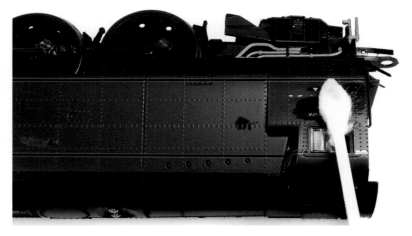

Each Pressfix numeral is removed by scoring through the upper paper carrier film and peeling individual numerals from the backing sheet. This is a different technique from that used for waterslide transfers, which are removed from the backing sheet by soaking them in water.

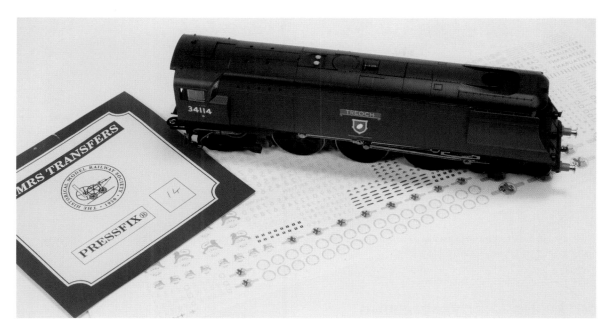

HMRS Pressfix transfers are ideal for this project because they offer enough numbers on one sheet to complete the project.

Once the renumbering is complete, the treated area is sprayed with matt varnish. Varnish protects the transfers and kills any unwanted glossiness from the paint and transfers. Masking tape provides protection for those areas of the model that do not need any attention.

The rear of each nameplate is roughened to provide a key for the adhesive.

The completed renumbering with new numerals applied seamlessly to the cab of the locomotives and new nameplates to create unique identities.

DETAILING AND WEATHERING OF A VITRAINS CLASS 47

One of the features of the ViTrains range of Class 37s and 47s is the number of models released over the course of a single year, offering a wider variety of liveries than is usually available from other sources. Even though both Hornby and Bachmann offer models of Class 47s, they are yet to provide the modeller with some popular up-to-date liveries such as the very contemporary Colas Rail scheme: bright, colourful and very well researched.

By retaining factory-applied liveries, the ViTrains Class 47 can be worked into a very authentic looking model with relatively little time and cost. The Class 47 comes with class- and locomotive-specific detail, making this task easier for the modeller, although there are many small but important refinements that can be made to the model. The result of about ten hours' work on the chosen subject for this project, Colas Rail 47 739, 'Robin of Templecombe', has produced very acceptable results that look great both on the layout and in a showcase. Careful weathering

ViTrains Class 47 models are worthy of consideration thanks to the variety of liveries regularly offered and the good proportions that capture the character of the full-size locomotives. While patience is required to fit the add-on parts, some minimalist detailing can lift the models to a new level without repainting.

and spot repainting of details such as buffer beams add character to what is otherwise a very plastic-looking model. However, the base material is good and that gives the modeller a fair chance of making something of a model that appears in a new livery at fairly regular intervals.

The work was completed in the following manner over a period of about four days to allow paint and adhesives to dry properly. Reference photographs were used to verify the precise details of 47 739.

- The supplied detailing parts were fitted to the bogies and bodyshell (using the techniques described in Chapter 2). These included the etched handrails and lamp irons.
- Hornby air pipe detail (as supplied in detail add-on packs with their new-generation diesel loco models) was used to detail the buffer beams because they are finer in appearance. A scale coupling was added to one end at the same time, while the other end of the model was fitted with a working coupling (a Kadee 'whisker' coupling) so it can pull trains on the layout.

- The appropriate details representing electric train supply jumper cables were added to the model.
- Etched nameplates and crests were used to cover the printed ones. Those printed on the model were found to be oversize, so the same technique used to remove locomotive numbers was used to reduce the size of the nameplates.
- The model of 47 739 was supplied with the correct buffer type, which could be reused on the model. I did, however, consider replacing them with Hornby Class 60 buffers, which are available as a spare and are far superior in appearance. In the end, those supplied with the model were glued into the headstocks and the buffer heads prevented from rotating with a spot of glue.
- Painting the wheels, weathering the roof with exhaust carbons (roof dirt) and underframe with brake dust will do much to tone down the plastic feel that ViTrains Class 47 models seem to have. All of the weathering colours are gently drifted onto the model with an airbrush to create dry dusting effects of brake dust and exhaust.

The base model (right), after fitting of the supplied detailing parts but before customization.

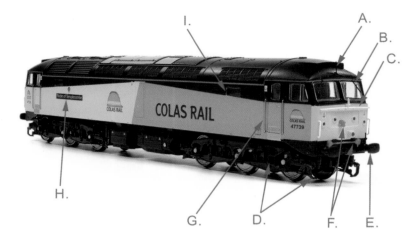

I. A. B. C.

H. G. D. F. E.

COLAS RAIL

COLAS RAIL
47739

47 739 after ten hours on the workbench and painting booth: (A) the aerials supplied with the model were fitted after checking that they are of the correct type; (B) windscreen wipers fitted, but note that the cab remains to be detailed; (C) the supplied handrails were applied and touched in with white paint; (D) bogie details applied using a glue suitable for hard shiny plastic; (E) the supplied buffers were retained and glued securely to the buffer beam; (F) multiple working and Electric Train Supply boxes and cables; (G) cab side handrails applied using those supplied with the model; (H) etched nameplates replace the printed ones; (I) look for paint shadows around windows and other details and touch in with an appropriate colour.

47802

Minor surgery is sometimes necessary as part of a minimalist project to add class-specific detail, as was the case with this ViTrains model of DRS 47 802. To avoid damaging the original paint finish, it is done with great care.

The printed nameplates were slightly too long to be covered by the etched plates supplied by Shawplan Models. IPA was used, in this instance, to remove part of the printing so the etched ones would cover them completely.

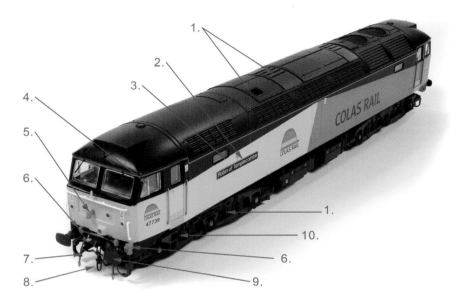

Another view of 47 739 with refinements and detailing complete, except for the cab interior: (1) weathering to roof, wheels and underframe; (2) new etched nameplates from Shawplan Models; (3) paint shadows around details and windows painted in; (4) cab glazing bar of black tape to be fitted to the cab side window; (5) multiple working socket fitted and painted orange; (6) Electric Train Supply (ETS) boxes fitted using supplied details and painted orange; (7) air brake and control pipes fitted using Hornby details; (8) Hornby screw link coupling bought as a spare fitted; (9) buffers supplied with the model reused, and glued to prevent them from rotating; (10) care taken to add detailing parts with a suitable glue so they do not become lost when the model is in service.

HORNBY CLASS 60 – A NEW IDENTITY

When a particular model has been released in a limited number of schemes, modellers are left with a bit of a challenge if uniformity is to be avoided. Only a limited number of Class 60 variants have been offered by Hornby since its release: the EW&S version used in this project is one of just four available by mid-January 2006. While things have improved with the release of some BR freight sector Class 60s, modellers are left with some work to represent other members of the 100-strong fleet.

Many simple techniques can be used to make the best of an existing livery. Renumbering the model is one way of giving it its own unique identity. Partial repainting to apply a unique feature is another. Weathering is the ultimate customization job because no two modellers will achieve exactly the same effect.

The Hornby Class 60 is very easy to dismantle thanks to a careful design that routes all of the wires along the chassis and not into the body. There are no screws to find and release: the body is secured to the chassis with simple retaining clips. The body was partially dismantled by removing the handrails and cab glazing. Once dismantled, work could start on removing the unwanted printed numbers and the EW&S logo. Don't forget that the number is repeated on the cab fronts. Some experimentation revealed that Slater's track cleaning fluid was the most effective solvent for removing the printed detail. However, its efficiency also meant that it readily attacked the varnish finish applied to the model and if cotton buds were rubbed too firmly against the model, it would remove the paint itself.

It did not take long to have a bodyshell bereft of any identification, ready for the application of a new identity and, in my case, new logos as well. Anyone

A welcome addition to any collection of modern, high horsepower freight diesels is the Hornby Class 60, first released at the end of 2005. A heavy chassis and all-wheel drive offer much-needed haulage capability for large layout owners who wish to run long trains. It makes an excellent companion for the Bachmann Class 66 and many of the recently released modern freight wagons now available from Bachmann and Hornby.

with good photographs of 60 026 will note that this locomotive was never adorned with the 'Three Beasties' logo on the cab. The model in that respect is accurate, which means that modellers will need to add that detail when changing the model's identity.

One detail that did not appear to be correct when I examined the model was the colour of the EWS gold band, which appears to be the same as that applied to the cab fronts (warning panel yellow). While there are slight differences in colour shade between individual locomotives due to variation between batches of paint or simply due to weathering and fading, the colour difference is not as marked as seen on the Hornby model. I first decided to partially repaint the model by masking off the gold line and applying Phoenix Precision EWS gold, protecting the rest of the model with masking tape and paper. Care was taken to mask over the etched side grilles to avoid the need to touch them in with black paint when partial repainting was complete.

An alternative method is to use Modelmaster Professional EWS gold transfer trim film from sheet number 4941, which is exactly the right width to cover the original paint applied to the Hornby model. It is a waterslide transfer, released from its

backing sheet by soaking in warm water and applied to the model carefully using a soft paintbrush to dab it into place without damaging it. Microscale setting solutions will help to seat it into place, especially around the engine room doors. What you are trying to achieve with this technique is the appearance of a neatly painted band of colour that will accept transfers for numbers and logos but without using any paint whatsoever. Leave it to set overnight before attempting to apply waterslide transfers from Fox Transfers sheet F4977/2. Any attempt to speed up the job by applying additional transfers before the gold band has properly set will result in the transfer being reactivated and spoiling all your hard work.

Now that job has been done, you must consider how to protect the waterslide transfers you have applied to change the model's identity. A coat of matt varnish is the safest and easiest way to do this. Varnishing also has the benefit of homogenizing the uneven finish that results from using different types of paint and/or waterslide transfers, which may have anything from a super gloss to a dead matt finish. You may choose to apply the matt varnish before you weather the model or after you have completed the job. Matt varnish also adds to the weathering effect by toning down the paint colours very slightly so that they appear to be bleached or faded. The fading effect can be exaggerated by adding a tiny touch of light grey paint to the varnish before spraying it, assuming that you are applying it with an airbrush.

A two-part weathering system was used on this model to pick out individual details in the first instance and to apply general weathering such as underframe dirt and exhaust carbons, which has the effect of toning down weathering effects applied directly with a paintbrush, sponge or rag.

Some details are best picked out by applying a thinned dark grey acrylic paint mix to areas of the model such as the engine room doors and roof panels. Paint can be applied with a paintbrush, running it into the door lines and seams that represent individual panels. Almost immediately after application it is wiped off, leaving behind a trace of colour that has become trapped in the seams and door lines.

It will also collect around raised detail, effectively highlighting it.

Direct weathering can also be applied using a dry-brushing technique. Dip the first few millimetres of your paintbrush directly into un-thinned paint and immediately wipe off the excess by rubbing it across a lint-free cloth until barely a trace of paint remains on the brush. Then brush over raised detail on the model, the raised detail catching what little paint remains in the brush. Sometimes this technique works well with light greys, sometimes with dark grey paint. Remember, with dry brushing, less is more. One secret I have learned is never to use black or white for this type of weathering, not even to represent coal dust. If you try Railmatch roof dirt as a weathering colour, which is a very dark grey shade and the enamel paint equivalent to Polly S 'dirty black', popular with US modellers, you will be surprised at how dark it appears when applied to the model.

The first task was to test the colour density of the chosen transfers that would eventually be used to renumber the model to provide it with a new identity. This project changes its identity from early EW&S branding to the revised style, which involves a change in the typeface as well as the logo.

Hornby has abandoned the use of body securing screws on its Class 60, relying on eight clips instead. This makes removal of the bodyshell very simple. The cab moulding and light circuit board assemblies are plugged into the inside faces of the cab fronts and are easily pushed out by inserting a screwdriver blade between the cab front and the moulding itself.

The objective is to retain as much of the original livery as possible, saving money and time by not fully repainting the model. Comparison with transfers and modelling paint shows that the gold stripe applied to the side of the model is not strictly of the correct shade for EWS livery. It can be corrected by partially repainting the model or by applying transfer trim film. Some of the materials required are shown in this image, including low tack masking tape, transfers for EWS livery and suitable paint.

Renumbering can be as simple and effortless as using a suitable solvent to remove the printed figures and replacing them with transfers of your choice.

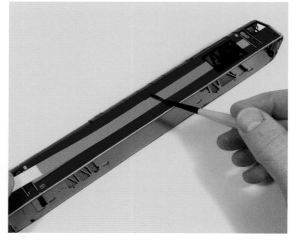

ABOVE: Modelmaster lining transfer is applied with a Microscale setting solution called Micro Sol, which helps the transfer to adhere to the model, especially over details such as door lines. The EWS gold lining being used in this image was taken from sheet 4941, which is of the correct width and was used to save a partial repaint. Once set, number transfers can be applied as if the surface was painted.

LEFT: Small pieces are cut to fit the area between bodyside grilles and the cab doors.

The buffers are sprung, which is a nice touch, especially if they do not rotate in the buffer shanks. Unfortunately, on the Hornby model they do rotate slightly. The simple cure is to glue them with a tiny quantity of varnish applied with a scalpel blade.

Open out the holes in the buffer beam to accept the air pipe detail supplied with the model. It also comes with additional mouldings for the fairing if the NEM coupling socket is not required.

The air pipes are plugged in with a minimal touch superglue to secure them.

Fox Transfers make all of its transfers as 'waterslide', designed to be immersed in warm water to detach the transfer from its backing paper before removal of excess water and application to the model.

The transfer stripe has dried sufficiently to add the new number transfers that will give the model its new identity.

As each transfer soaks in warm water, you will notice that it shows signs of detaching from the backing paper after a few minutes. Before it becomes completely detached, remove it from the water and place it on kitchen towel. Wait until all excess water has been absorbed by the kitchen towel before use.

If you position a transfer in the wrong place, quickly apply water to release it from the painted surface and then reposition it using the paintbrush. Excess water can be absorbed by touching it with a corner from a sheet of kitchen towel. When satisfied with the position of the transfer, press it gently but firmly into place.

The action of wiping off the excess weathering paint works it into seams, door lines, nooks and crannies. Dark grey colours usually give a better result than black paint.

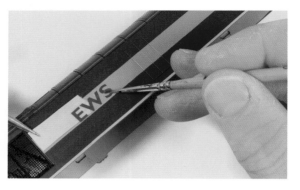

Waterslide transfers are generally delicate and should be eased off the backing paper and into place with a clean paintbrush.

Weathering is an excellent method of further customizing a ready-to-run product. On this project, door lines were roughly picked out with dark grey paint before the excess was immediately wiped off.

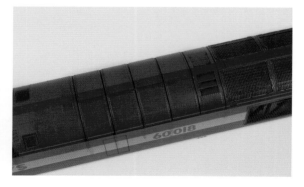

The locomotive roof has been subjected to weathering using a two-part process that commenced with the wipe-off method to highlight body detail and was finished with airbrushed weathering to apply exhaust carbons along the roof and around the large exhaust silencers.

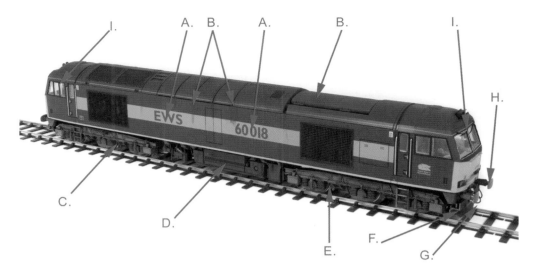

Two evenings of work have resulted in a very different looking model. Examining it critically, I would choose to apply less weathering to the body sides next time. The application of a coat of matt varnish has removed differences in the finish of the model caused by spot painting and the application of transfers. Paint applied to door lines and engine room panels is toned down by varnish and exhaust colour dusted on with an airbrush. Details to note: (A) New locomotive number and herald applied using water slide transfers. (B) Weathering applied with roof dirt paint colour. (C) Brake dust dusted onto the under frames and bogies. (D) Oil staining to fuel tanks. (E) Wheels are painted and weathered. (F) Fairing glued firmly in place and weathered. (G) Air brake pipes. (H) Buffers glued to prevent them from rotating. (I) Metal window frame represented with silver paint.

The chosen subject for the Hornby Class 60 project is 60 018, an unassuming locomotive without any identifying features or nameplates. It was photographed south of Leicester, coasting downgrade from Kibworth summit towards Wigston South Junction with empty Bardon Stone hoppers on 12 July 2004.

MINIMAL REPAINTING OF SHUNTING LOCOMOTIVES

One way of saving a considerable amount of time repainting Class 08 shunters is to retain the yellow and black stripes on both ends of the bodyshell. I usually mask these off very carefully, paying particular attention to the edge of the masking tape to prevent paint creeping underneath it and then apply a new body colour such as gloss rail blue to the base model that was to become 08 567. This is a very simple way of painting locomotive bodies. The way in which the Hornby model is assembled is particularly useful because the cab can be treated separately from the main bodyshell. Some masking tape will also need to be applied to the cab mouldings, and cab interior detail such as drivers' stools are better removed and replaced after painting and detailing are finished, because you can guarantee they will break off at some stage of the project if you don't.

The most effective way of improving a Hornby Class 08 (or Class 09) is through weathering and the addition of locomotive-specific details for a given time in its life. In the case of the model of 08 567, I paid particular attention to the locomotive markings, which place the livery very much in the BR blue era but also bring it forward to about 2003 with modern electrification warning notices.

My reference slides were initially examined for details under a magnifying glass on a light table. It was only after acquiring a high-quality scanner, however, and scanning the same slides so that the images could be examined on-screen that I noticed a couple of details I had not applied to the model. The first one was that the cab handrails are painted black and not white. The second detail I missed was that the cab roof hatch had been removed and plated over. Both of these details can be applied retrospectively to the model but it does show that careful examination of reference photographs is quite important.

When undertaking such a project, the modeller should pay particular attention to the following:

- The underframe of most shunters of this type becomes quite oily and greasy after a period of time. Weathering is likely to be more oil and grease than brake dust because these locomotives rarely get out onto the main line and never travel at a speed sufficient to generate quantities of brake dust. Areas of the underframe affected include the phosphor bronze pickups, which are just visible through the outside frames, the ends of the extended cranks and the coupling rods themselves.
- Weathering can do a great deal to add character to these models. It can take the form of

Hornby's model of 08 528 provided the base model for my attempt at 08 567. Before it was repainted, various printed details, such as the legend 'Liverpool Street Station Pilot', were removed so they would not strike through the new coat of paint.

rust patches on the cab roof, rust and exhaust carbons around the exhaust manifold located to the front of the bonnet, sun bleaching of the paint (these locomotives are rarely repainted and rarely stored under cover) and grease on various panels and equipment boxes.

- Take advantage of the detailing parts supplied with the model. I am particularly keen on the use of the Hornby air pipe detail because it is made from flexible plastic that is less prone to breakage and more durable than white metal ones.

- The Hornby 08 shunter is very easy to repaint if care is taken to mask the yellow and black striped ends. This saves a considerable amount of time, yet is an important step to customizing

This is the finished result after around 20 hours of workbench time. Despite careful initial examination of slides under a magnifying glass, there are two details that need to be corrected on the finished model so that it matches the full-size locomotive.

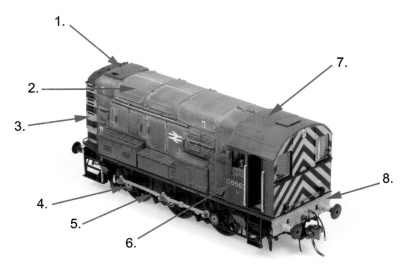

Weathering applied to the model of 08 567 includes rusting of the exhaust panel (1) and bleaching to the bonnet, which was achieved by mixing rail grey and rail blue to create a lighter shade of paint (2) that was then applied to the base coat of rail blue using make-up sponges rather than a paintbrush. The original stripes painted on the model by Hornby were retained (3). More black and dark grey paint could be applied to underframe detail to represent the oil and grime that builds up on these locomotives (4), particularly on coupling rods (5). Transfers were selected from HMRS Pressfix sheet No. 15 (6) (also available on NMS Sheet 1) and rust weathering applied to the cab roof (7). The buffer beam was painted yellow at the cab end only (8).

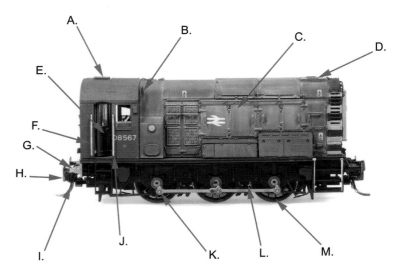

Detailing that may be applied to the Hornby model includes: (A) the cab roof vent remains to be replaced but was retrospectively removed, based on photographic evidence; (B) the whistle may be replaced by a warning horn on some locomotives; (C) sun bleaching of paint on the bonnet doors and top; (D) exhaust panel is treated with rust coloured paint; (E) leave the cab doors open to reveal the lovely cab interior; (F) handrails are not always painted white; (G) look for replacement buffers, sometimes applied to one end only; (H) Kadees can make shunting operations more enjoyable and are easy to fit to NEM coupling pockets; (I) fit the air pipes supplied in the box and weather them; (J) improve the cab interior with a driver, tail lamps and other kit; (K) apply weathering to coupling rods and outside cranks with black or dark grey paint; (L) apply black paint to the phosphor bronze pickup strip in order to kill the shine; (M) fitting Ultrascale wheels to the Hornby Class 08 shunter is an excellent way to upgrade the model.

a model to such an extent that it becomes very much part of your personal collection and not just another box from the model shop.

- The Hornby Class 08 model features sprung cab doors that may be opened but always slam themselves shut on one's fingers. A little character can be added to the model by removing the spring from the door so that it opens and closes freely on its hinges. Why not apply a tiny quantity of glue to the door so that it is held in an open position, and then add some detail to the already superbly decorated cab interior, including a kit bag, driver and another of those tail lamps produced by Springside Models?

- Shunting locomotives invariably collect a small cargo of equipment relating to their role in freight yards and carriage sidings. Why not add some simple details such as a shunter's pole and tail lamps? Both details are produced in

4mm scale by Springside Models, including the earlier BR oil lamp and the later battery-operated flashing tail-light.

MINIMAL DETAILING OF A LIMITED EDITION BACHMANN CLASS 57

A limited edition model of the unique Class 57, No. 57 601, was produced by Bachmann in 2009 and all but sold out within months. Exclusive models do not normally make suitable projects for detailing and enhancement, at least not according to collectors! This model was a fairly good representation of the full-size locomotive, which is operated today by West Coast Railway Company of Carnforth.

Examination of reference photographs, however, showed that a couple of details fitted to the model were not correct. The model was supplied with sand boxes on the bogies, which were removed, and part of the underframe boxes was missing too. The fitting of Hornby buffer beam pack air brake pipes and

LEFT: **The full-size 57 601 was photographed passing through Nairn with the 'Royal Scotsman' in August 2007. This is a useful reference photograph.**

BELOW: **The Bachmann model of 57 601 was released as a limited edition model for** Model Rail **magazine. The model is shiny and pristine, making it ideal for weathering and some small measure of detailing.**

BELOW: **The model is in need of some refinement to remove the surplus sand boxes from the bogies, tidy up the wonky buffers and remove the too bright finish.**

Bachmann jumper cables, together with weathering and detail painting, soon saw the model ready for service. The project was undertaken in a few hours on the workbench and paint shop. There was no renumbering and renaming required of the model to match a full-size locomotive and the livery was not overpainted in any way. Small corrections, detailing and weathering was all this project amounted to. It demonstrates how an out-of-the-box locomotive can be detailed and made unique to you when you are happy with the choice of livery and number.

CONCLUSION

The projects in this chapter demonstrate how the often shiny and pristine models we buy straight from the box can be enhanced to improve their appearance to some extent, either to disguise the plastic feel of some or to make others look like their hard-worked, full-size counterparts. The next chapter looks at simple but effective techniques for maintaining the environment in which our models are expected to work: the layout itself. Track cleaning, maintenance and fine tuning the layout is described next, a vital part of keeping our prized models running as smoothly as possible.

Replacement wheels (Black Beetle) to EM gauge were fitted using the techniques described in Chapter 3. Note that the wheel faces are painted in underframe dirt colour, ready for when the model is weathered.

The brake shoes and hangers were loose in the model upon receipt. To prevent fouling of the new EM gauge wheels, some plastic was snipped away with Xuron shears.

Plastic Weld liquid poly cement was used to fit the trimmed brake show mouldings to the inside of the bogie frames (after the frames were cleaned of oil)

Off with those sand boxes – but do it carefully with a scalpel to prevent unwanted damage.

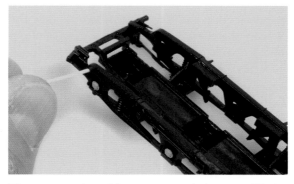

The unwanted sand box mounting holes were filled with styrene rod and painted.

Electric Train Supply jumper cables and boxes provided with the model are fitted. The boxes are spot painted orange. The boxes were first prepared with grey primer, which prevents the black plastic from striking through and gives the light orange colour a good base for even coverage.

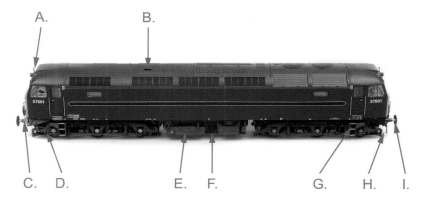

The model with detailing and weathering completed: (A) cab aerials replaced with fine wire; (B) inside edges of exhaust ports painted black and surround sprayed with roof dirt colour to represent exhaust; (C) buffer beam details painted with appropriate colours; (D) sand boxes removed; (E) fuel tank details checked and streaked with grime as part of the weathering process; (F) missing electrical equipment box made up from strips of 10 thou black styrene; (G) detail painting, with dull steel colour added to bogie footsteps; (H) air brake pipes fitted to the buffer beams using parts from a spare Hornby add-on pack; (I) detail painting, with dull steel colour added to buffer shanks.

Toning down the underframes with weathering and adding buffer beam details both enhance the model and bring it to life. Gone is the pristine limited edition model straight from the box and the simple enhancement makes it more at home on a scenic layout.

A visit to Kyle of Lochalsh for 57 601 in August 2006 with the 'Royal Scotsman' presented a number of photographic opportunities. This view taken from the road bridge at the station shows the weathering to the roof and underframes.

CHAPTER SIX

KEEPING THE LAYOUT RUNNING SMOOTHLY

The full-size railways use specialized vehicles in right of way maintenance, for example for weed spraying and for the application of Sandite during leaf fall season and de-icing fluid to conductor rails on frosty nights. In the UK, Multiple Purpose Vehicles such as DR98974 work with interchangeable modules consisting of liquid storage tanks and spray equipment on weed-killing and Sandite trains in the same manner as a modeller may run a track cleaning car around the layout to keep things running smoothly.

INTRODUCTION

When a layout is displayed at public exhibitions or used for regular operating sessions with friends or club members, smooth running is vital to the enjoyment of the audience viewing the layout or the operating session. There is nothing worse than a poor performing layout, whether it is an exhibition layout designed to be transported to public shows or one that lives permanently at home. Having to constantly prod reluctant trains into action detracts from the time and effort put into building a scale model. Most modellers do an excellent job of constructing baseboards and laying track, together with completing the electronics to make it all work. Poor performance can be more attributed to dirty track, damage, fluff, hairs and other causes because we cannot keep our models together with the layouts they run on in sterile conditions. They are exposed

to dust, hairs from pets, humidity and various other environmental considerations that will very much depend on where the layout is stored and used.

Speak to any modeller exhibiting their layout at a public show and the topic of conversation will soon turn to methods of achieving smooth running and reliable control, which is particularly important when you are displaying your pride and joy for the paying public. There are numerous techniques, tricks of the trade if you like, used to keep it all running satisfactorily. It can be particularly challenging to maintain smooth performance on exhibition layouts because they are regularly dismantled and assembled, and then jiggled about in the back of a car or van when transported to and from exhibition halls. Maintenance becomes of paramount importance as small details become loosened or broken, rail ends bend and buckle, and wires and soldered joints come loose.

I have experience of operating three exhibition layouts of my own, as well as numerous club layouts, and employ a basic routine for cleaning and maintenance of the layout before it is loaded into the car and transported to a show. The same techniques can be used to prepare a permanent home-based layout for an operating evening with friends, or a club layout for an open evening or operating night. The techniques are simple and may vary depending on the preferences of individual modellers. They have worked very well for me in the past and I hope they will provide some assistance in helping you achieve the same smooth and reliable running that I expect from my own exhibition layouts. A couple of hours of preparation will save much embarrassment and frustration when the serious running of trains commences.

Essential tools and materials for layout maintenance include track and wheel gauges, a fibreglass pencil, scrapers, coupling gauges and a paintbrush for dusting (and nothing else). Isopropyl alcohol (IPA) is an excellent solvent for track and wheel cleaning. Avoid using methylated spirits, because experience shows that it leaves a residue behind that hinders electrical conductivity.

Use the same back-to-back gauges employed to check the wheels of your model locomotives to measure the wheels of wagons and coaches too. It is sometimes easier to remove wheel sets from wagons and coaching stock for inspection and placing in a gauge.

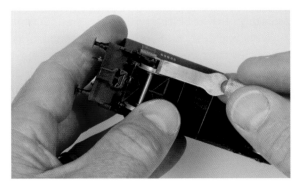

Rolling stock wheels pick up dirt, too, and that should be cleaned away as a part of the routine maintenance and cleaning work.

CHECK THE RAIL GAUGE AND EXAMINE THE TRACK

Examining the permanent way is something that is regularly undertaken by the full-size railways to ensure that safety standards are upheld. Theoretically, your own examination of the layout is therefore quite prototypical and will pay dividends in smooth running and realistic operations.

Unfortunately, and particularly on exhibition layouts, track can become damaged. This might happen during transportation or if a heavy object, such as a tool, is dropped on it. Soldered joints also become loose from time to time, contributing to derailments that probably take place at locations where you would least expect them. Even when the track is in perfectly good condition, daft things can cause derailments, such as stray pieces of ballast lodged between switch rails and stock rails in turnouts, or jammed between the running rail and check rails.

It is worth making a quick examination of the track from time to time using a pair of fine-nose tweezers to remove pieces of stray ballast that may otherwise cause problems. At the same time, look out for fabric fluff, pet hairs or even tiny shavings of styrene left over from the last modelling project on the layout. This detritus seems to get everywhere and you can guarantee that it will cause derailments at the very first opportunity. If it doesn't derail the locomotive, it is guaranteed to get caught up in the mechanism, setting in motion a whole different set of problems, such as binding of the gears (see Chapter 7), wear and tear, or poor electrical conductivity between wheels and pickups.

Suspect areas of track can be checked with a track gauge to see if the gauge measurement is correct. Trouble spots are usually identified by random items of rolling stock derailing regularly at the same location, time and time again. Gauges can take the form of roller gauges or flat gauges such as that supplied by Peco as part of its Individulay track component range. Also look for misaligned rail joints where the ends of the rail may show vertical or horizontal displacement of more than a fraction of a millimetre.

Run your finger along the rail to check for burrs left over from cutting the rail during track laying, both on the top running surface and on the side of the rail. Smooth away rough edges with grade 1200 wet and dry paper, which is very fine and won't damage the rail top if used gently. Run it along the length of the rail and not across it, and do not be too heavy with it so as to avoid damaging the rail top.

CLEAN THE TRACK

Dirty track has to be one of the most frustrating problems that modellers face on a regular basis, particularly on large layouts. As dust settles on the rails between operating sessions, and as oil accumulates with other dirt during operating sessions, electrical conductivity between wheels and rail deteriorates to the point where reliable current supply to the motor and onboard systems is no longer possible. The result is inevitable: jerky running, flashing lights and disappointingly poor performance. This is particularly frustrating when operation involves slow speed running, such as shunting with tank engines, diesel electric Class 08s and 09s or other short locomotives.

The answer to this problem is very simple: clean the track! Many modellers get terribly concerned about methods of track cleaning and there are quite a few opinions on how this can be done reliably. First check if your track is dirty by using the white cloth test: do this before trains have a chance to really spread it around the layout and before it affects train performance. Take a piece of white kitchen towel and simply run it along the rails. If it picks up what appears to be dark grey greasy muck, it is safe to assume the track needs cleaning.

I use several methods to clean track, or more specifically the rails, depending on the circumstances. If the layout has not been used for a period of time, tarnish is likely to be a problem. My preferred method of dealing with this is to use a fibreglass stick very gently on the rail surface and the inside edge too, because model locomotives will pick up electrical current from both the side and the top of the rail. A second method is to use a lint-free cloth soaked with isopropyl alcohol (IPA). This is very efficient at removing oil and dirt from the rail without scouring it unnecessarily. Alcohol and cloth is the gentlest method of cleaning your track.

Very dirty rails can be rubbed down with a track rubber, but choose these with care because some are very abrasive. While they appear to offer a very simple and straightforward method of track cleaning, many of them scrub the surface of the rail quite aggressively and this can wear down the top of the rail after a while. Some commercial turnouts, such as Insulfrog turnouts produced by Peco, can become damaged by the overuse of track rubbers. If a track rubber is your preferred method of cleaning track, choose one that is relatively soft to the touch and does not have a coarse texture.

Owners of large layouts will find the day-to-day cleaning of the track a fairly onerous job and dealing with large permanent home layouts with 50 linear feet or more of main running line becomes a chore. This raises an interesting point. Day-to-day maintenance should be given careful consideration when the layout is going through the concept and design stage. Will you be able to cope with the amount of track when it comes to maintenance and cleaning? Don't forget that this will be in addition to caring for the wheels, pickups and couplings of the large amount of stock required to populate it effectively.

Fortunately there are products available that make the cleaning of track less demanding. As an enthusiastic DCC-user, I have an instant dislike of high-frequency electronic track cleaners, which can do a considerable amount of damage to decoders and command stations. The solution is to use a track cleaning car and there are several available that have very good reputations for performance. Some are designed to be filled with track cleaning solvent and either pushed or hauled by a locomotive around the layout until all the track has been cleaned. The cleaning action is achieved through a steady stream of solvent fed to a soft pad on the underside of the track cleaning car as it is used. A popular model available in N, HO/OO and O gauge is the CMX 'Clean Machine': its brass construction makes it completely immune to the effects of track cleaning solvent. There are similar track cleaning cars that rely on abrasive action on the rails and these too are very successful. UK-outline modellers will find the track cleaning car conversion kit by LMS of particular interest as it is based on a roller mechanism that fits a Hornby LMS brake van. Whichever track cleaning car you choose to buy, they are extremely useful in those situations where bridges, tunnels, overhead line equipment and signals may make the manual cleaning of track difficult.

The white glove test: if your track is clean, only the barest amount of dirt will be picked up by a clean cotton glove when rubbed across the surface of running rails.

Dirt collected from the rails using disposable kitchen paper towel soaked with IPA.

Using a fibreglass scratch stick to shift more stubborn dirt. Rub along the length of the rail and not across it, and do not forget to clean the inside rail edges too.

Choose a gentle track rubber such as this rubbing block offered by C&L Finescale. Track rubbers can abrade the track if used with too much vigour.

Abrasive paper has its uses when removing burrs from cut rail ends. Use gently and along the rails, not across them to prevent cross-scoring of the rail head.

Examine flange ways and the space between switch rails and stock rails for stray ballast and other detritus. A turnout undergoes its periodical inspection to check that the switch blades move smoothly and there is nothing preventing them from closing correctly.

All seems to be well with this turnout. The switch rail closes right up to the stock rail, leaving no gap that could cause a derailment.

Roller gauges are used to check the track on a layout, measuring the distance between the rails. They are great for checking trouble spots where rolling stock regularly derails. Derailments are usually due to unwanted gauge widening or narrowing, a fault that a roller gauge will soon reveal.

Track gauges can come in the form of a flat metal plate, such as this one produced by Peco. They do the same job as a roller gauge and can also be used to check flange way clearances on turnouts.

This image illustrates two important points regarding the smooth operation of a layout. When designing and building a layout, be sure to set adequate clearances with your longest items of rolling stock. During routine maintenance, look out for detritus left over from modelling projects (indicated by the red arrow). Remove by vacuuming or with tweezers, watching out for any parts that may have fallen off locomotives or rolling stock.

THE DCC AND DIRTY TRACK MYTH

While on the subject of dirty rails and poor performance, a commonly quoted myth is that layouts using Digital Command Control systems will only function properly if the track is 'particularly clean'. Having discussed this with a number of people to determine what the term 'particularly clean' actually means in real life, I have concluded that this is definitely one of those wonderful 'shaggy dog' stories that circulate around the hobby. Based on my own experience of using various DCC systems, I can only conclude that rails are either dirty or they're not. I am not entirely sure how one can make the surface of rails 'particularly' or 'extra' clean. I take no more precaution over the cleaning of the rails on my DCC exhibition layouts than I have ever done when operating analogue layouts. Dirt on the rails affects analogue and digital control in equal measure and good cleanliness in both cases is one of the solutions to achieving trouble-free operation.

CLEAN ROLLING STOCK WHEELS

While you're busy cleaning the track and have the tools and materials to hand, consider examining the wheels of locomotives and rolling stock to see how much dirt has accumulated on them. Rolling stock wheels very quickly build up a layer of grime that can, in the finer scales, actually cause derailments as the effect of a finer flange is further reduced by dirt. Dirt also causes irregular running with rolling stock and that looks awful on a layout as the models run erratically. Rolling stock wheels are easy to clean with a fibreglass pencil or, if the soiling is not too bad, isopropyl alcohol on a lint-free cloth. Serious build-up of dirt should be removed using a modelling knife chisel blade, being careful to avoid scratching the wheel surface, which will only encourage the accumulation of more dirt.

COUPLING HEIGHT AND POSITION ON ROLLING STOCK

While it is unlikely that the operating height of couplings on locomotives and rolling stock is affected

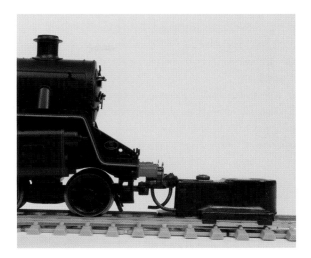

The use of a gauge to check the position of couplings is very good practice. Most coupling manufacturers offer a gauge specific to their products: the No. 205 height gauge by Kadee is demonstrated in this photograph.

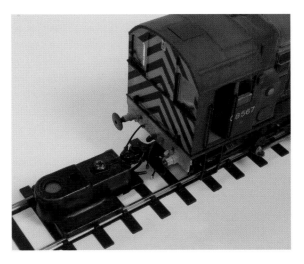

Looking down on the Kadee coupling gauge, this time being used to check the couplings clipped into the NEM362 coupling boxes fitted to this Hornby model.

on a day-to-day basis, some types of coupling used by finescale modellers are more prone to damage than others. It is useful to have at least one coupling height gauge to hand on the workbench to examine the height of couplings, which will also indicate if they have been damaged. A single misaligned coupling on one wagon within a train can be enough to cause irritating derailments on curves and junctions.

My preferred coupling is the American-made Kadee. On this type the height at which the couplings are fitted is critical for smooth operation and the use of uncoupling magnets. Checking the height of any couplings and ensuring that all of the parts are free moving and complete will do much to improve the running of your layout.

CHECK FOR OBSTRUCTIONS AND CLEARANCE

I recently witnessed an interesting occurrence when testing a train of passenger coaches on one part of a club layout. For some strange reason, the train would become uncoupled halfway down the rake and there was no obvious explanation. This fault occurred time and time again, but not every time the train passed that point on the layout. After an hour of this, the spot where the fault occurred was carefully examined and it was found that one of the retaining bolts used as part of the baseboard construction was close to the running line and on a slight curve. This was enough to catch the overhang of one of the coaches and to lift it sufficiently to disengage the couplings. While this did not occur on the scenic part of the layout, constantly having to stop the train to re-couple coaches became annoying and disrupted the smooth flow of the operating session. The problem was solved by two minutes' work with a file and it never reoccurred.

The lesson from that particular incident is to check new rolling stock to see that it fits all of the clearances, such as platform edges, signals and other details likely to be located close to the track, not to mention the baseboard structures, before subjecting it to a formal running session. After completing new work on the layout, it is also worth testing the longest item of rolling stock through that part of the layout to ensure that clearances have been maintained. Platform edges can be a particular problem to some modern rolling stock, including Mk.3 coaches

and modern era multiple units such as Turbostars and Class 158s.

EXAMINE WIRING

It is generally good practice when building a layout to ensure that each length of rail has an electrical feed supplying power to it, so as not to be relying on rail joiners to conduct electricity around the layout. This is particularly important with DCC, where electrical supply should be designed to ensure there is no voltage drop at the extreme ends of the layout. Reliable power supply is vital for exhibition layouts. Before any one of my portable layouts is loaded into the car for transport to an exhibition, everything is carefully checked to ensure that none of the wiring or droppers between track and the main wiring bus has become dislodged or disconnected.

Damage like this is so much less convenient to repair at the exhibition hall. It is better to make such repairs at home and take a reliable layout to the show than to undertake electrical repairs in the exhibition hall. The time available for setting up a layout at the start of a show should be used for adjusting it to the hall floor, ensuring that its presentation is as good as it possibly could be, and placing the rolling stock on the layout and ensuring it all runs smoothly. Using part of that time to make repairs to wiring is just frustrating.

BASEBOARD JOINTS AND ALIGNMENT

Some modellers who rely on the use of G-clamps for bolting a portable layout together, without any form of alignment, find that they slip during an exhibition, resulting in slight misalignment of the rails and the inevitable deterioration of performance. The use of pattern makers' dowels saves a great deal of time in aligning the baseboards during setup and makes the baseboard joints themselves that much more reliable, ensuring that performance is maintained. While some time may be saved during layout construction in avoiding the use of alignment techniques such as dowels, in the long term their use is considered to be

As portable layouts are used and transported, rail ends at baseboard joints can become misaligned after running repairs or through rough handling. The rail joints shown here are unacceptably misaligned and will need attention soon.

good practice. I would never build a portable exhibition layout without them.

Returning to the subject of portable layouts, baseboard joints can have a serious effect on reliability. Owners of permanent home layouts that are not designed to be portable may consider themselves fortunate. Baseboard joints are one of those necessary evils that cannot be avoided with portable layouts. Even using pattern makers' dowels, the constant set-up and breakdown of portable layouts can eventually move them out of alignment. Alignment can also be affected as the layout becomes older and the wood used to construct baseboards changes subtly, which will inevitably happen over a period of time.

Part of the longer-term maintenance regime for my portable layouts is to examine the baseboard joints and ensure that the pattern makers' dowels are still doing their job. When misalignment occurs, there are two ways of fixing it. The best method is to remove the dowels and reinstall them in a different

position at the baseboard joint after the baseboards have been correctly aligned once again and secured with G-clamps before drilling pilot holes. If the realignment has been discovered after setting up at the exhibition hall, and there appears to be no way of correcting it by adjusting the baseboard joint, the quick and dirty method would be to unsolder the rail ends and make realignments that way. This method may cause problems in the long term by introducing a slight but significant kink in the track that could become an area of unreliability in the future.

LAYOUT MAINTENANCE CHECK LIST

- Clean the track rails regularly at intervals of about once a month, depending on the environment the layout is stored in. If left for some time, clean the rails before operating.
- Vacuum dust from the layout, particularly from the track so that fluff is not picked up by locomotives and dust is not allowed to cover everything, including the rails.
- Note any poorly performing locomotives and stock and remove them from the layout for workbench attention.
- Check the coupling height on all stock regularly to ensure smooth shunting operations.
- Clean the wheels of locomotives and stock. The interval between cleaning will depend on how frequently the layout is run.
- Identify track trouble spots where rolling stock derails frequently in order to find the cause of the problem.
- Identify and remove stock that derails in random locations. Check the wheels for dirt and the gauge with a back-to-back gauge.
- Lubricate anything that squeaks or squeals!
- Inspect rail joints and baseboard joints on portable layouts for misalignment that could cause derailments.
- Inspect turnouts to see that the switch rails move smoothly when the points are changed and that they sit close to the stock rails when required to do so.

CONCLUSION

Layout, locomotive and rolling stock maintenance can be a bit of a chore. Cleaning track is definitely a chore, cleaning wheels can be painful and making sure that wiring, baseboard joints and scenery are not going to affect the smooth running of your layout is something that just has to be done. The best-running layouts that I have seen at exhibitions, however, are operated by modellers who go to extraordinary lengths to ensure that performance is maintained. The techniques in this chapter are just some of the methods regularly employed in exhibition halls, clubrooms and layout rooms up and down the country.

The old saying, 'five minutes in preparation saves fifteen minutes in execution', applies to model railways just as much as anything else in life. The reward will be good performance, smooth operations and a great deal of fun instead of frustration. The same applies to routine locomotive maintenance, which is the subject of the next chapter, together with undertaking repairs.

Back-to-back gauges can be used to check the wheels of rolling stock as well as locomotives. Making this part of your routine will also help to deal with misbehaving wagons and coaches that derail in random places on the layout when others do not.

Good layout maintenance and cleaning will make slow speed operations more enjoyable when the locomotives run through the track without hesitation and stalling. Keep the track clean and shunters will run slowly and smoothly as they work wagons to and fro in a yard like this.

CHAPTER SEVEN

ONGOING MAINTENANCE AND REPAIRS

Cleaning 'Oliver Cromwell', the Britannia Class locomotive built by BR in 1951 and now part of the National Collection, is well under way as the locomotive rests between steam charter trains in Scotland. Modellers may do a similar task by removing dust and fingerprints from the surfaces of models using a clean one-inch paintbrush dedicated to the task of dusting and a soft lint-free cloth.

INTRODUCTION

To conclude this manual of maintenance and fine tuning, this chapter contains practical advice on routine maintenance and repair. Some elements of maintenance, such as lubrication and wheel cleaning, have already been touched upon and those sections should be read in conjunction with this concluding chapter. Maintenance does not need to be onerous, so don't put it off, because five minutes of careful cleaning and lubrication will save much more time in repair and remedial work later. Some of my models can run for a very long time without a second's attention, thanks to the high reliability of contemporary standard models. Every six months or so, however, I work through my active fleet of locomotives to clean wheels, check the current collection

pickups and the level of lubrication on bearings and gears, regardless of whether the model is running smoothly or not. I sometimes find it surprising what details have fallen off in service and have to be prepared to replace missing air and vacuum brake pipes, footsteps, coupling hooks and even glazing. Glazing usually falls inside the bodyshell, so give the model a shake to hear if it's ratting around inside, just in case it gets into moving parts. Make a search along the permanent way of your layout, too, because many missing parts can be found on the ballast!

Rolling stock is left to its own devices until a fault develops. Always remove faulty equipment to the workbench as soon as a problem is detected, so as not to impair layout performance. By removing it straight away, you know it needs repair. Make a note in your defect book to ensure the repair is done and 'red card' it as necessary so your operators do not inadvertently pick it up and place it back on the layout.

The following twelve-point check list covers the key maintenance requirements for most contemporary standard models:

- Clean wheels, including the tyres and the inside faces where current collection pickups come into contact.
- Remove dirty grease and relubricate the gears, bearings and motor spindle with sparing amounts of oil.
- Clean and adjust pickups and associated contacts to ensure electricity flows without interruption.
- Search for and remove fabric fluff and pet hairs, which is often found wrapped around axles!
- Clean oil and grease from the inside of bodyshells.
- Replace broken couplings.
- Replace damaged or missing detailing parts.
- Inspect the wheels for damage and check the back-to-back measurements with a gauge.
- Inspect traction tyres for wear and replace with new ones if necessary.
- Inspect carbon brushes and springs if the motor design allows for such maintenance.
- Check electrical connections within the model and solder loose wires back into place.
- Brush away dust and remove fingerprints, oil and grease from the model's bodyshell.

Slow running and tight control is a feature of micro and end-to-end layouts where continuous running at speed is not possible. A yard environment calls for slow speed operations with shunting engines. The slower the pace, the more important the need for clean wheels, well-maintained mechanisms and reliable current collection between the rails and the motor.

Some useful materials for model cleaning and maintenance. They include fine mechanism or clock oil, micro-grease, tweezers for removing fluff and a fibreglass scratch pencil for wheel and electrical contact cleaning.

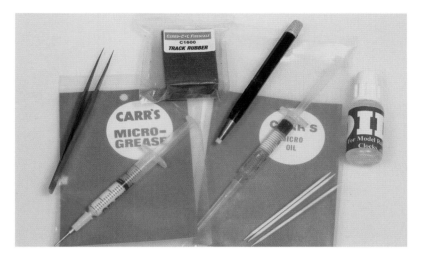

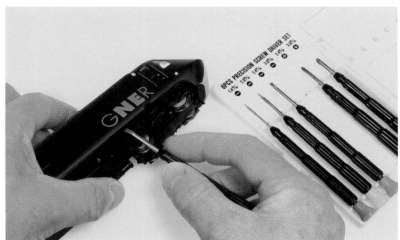

Knowing how to safely remove the bodyshells from models is essential to a maintenance regime. Have a set of precision jewellers' screwdrivers to hand for removing locomotive bodies. Use scraps of styrene card to hold the body away from body securing clips. For example, four screws hold the body on this Hornby GNER HST power car. The service sheets will show where screws and body clips are located on models.

Cleaning the current collection pickups of a Hornby HST power car with IPA and a soft cloth. This task should be applied to trailer vehicles with lighting circuits as well as the powered cars.

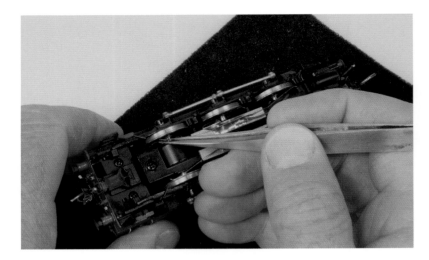

Inspect the current collection pickups to see that they actually make contact with the wheels. Adjust with pliers so that gentle pressure is brought to bear.

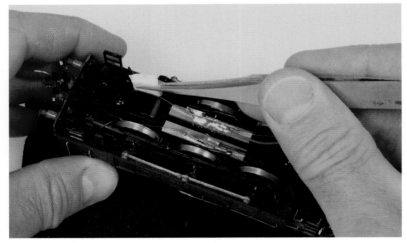

Clean the current collection pickups and the contact surface on the wheel tyre by gently inserting a piece of cloth or tissue soaked with IPA between the wheel and pickups.

Don't be afraid to dig around under circuit boards and other fittings to find bearings and couplings that need checking for wear and regular lubrication, not to mention parts that have fallen into the bodyshell.

PICKUPS

The majority of locomotives still use basic wiper pickups composed either of phosphor bronze strip or nickel silver wire to conduct current from the wheels to locomotives' internal wiring. Part of the locomotive maintenance plan should include examining the pickups to see that they are making contact with the back of the wheel without applying too much pressure, which could ultimately wear them out or cause an irritating scraping noise – or both! Dirt, fluff and hairs also accumulate between wiper pickups and the back of the wheel, which can cause erratic running and poor electrical conductivity. Remove stray fluff with tweezers and clean the pickups by inserting a piece of cloth or tissue soaked in isopropyl alcohol between the wheel and pickup: this usually removes most of the dirt.

CAREFUL LUBRICATION

Lubricants can dry out very quickly when a model has not been used for some time. Even brand new models may be lacking in lubricant if they have been sitting on the shelf at the shop longer than normal. It is worth checking how much lubrication there is on locomotive axles, cranks, coupling rods and gears to see that there is sufficient to prevent excessive wear and tear, not to mention unwanted mechanism noise. It is worth noting that excessive lubrication, which sometimes occurs with off-the-shelf models, is also undesirable because this can be flicked around the inside of the bodyshell making a mess and eventually depositing it on the track, which prevents good electrical conductivity.

Several types are lubricant are available, all of which are suitable for plastic models. Companies that offer lubricants for use with model railways take particular care to ensure that the oil or grease does not attack plastics. They are usually supplied in a handy applicator, which ensures that the minute quantities required to keep the mechanism ticking along smoothly are not exceeded. The brands of model oil and specialized 'moly grease' I use regularly are produced under the Carr's label by C&L Finescale or the Hob-e-Lube label. They are all plastic safe and have low shear characteristics for delicate mechanisms. They will also resist flicking around the inside of a model when the motor is rotating at high speed. Take care when choosing lubricants: the additional cost of those formulated for models is worth paying.

When lubricating models, do so very sparingly. Do not apply oil straight from a bottle in order to avoid flooding gears and the motor. Grease should be applied as a very thin smear and not in huge gobs. A little of both goes a very long way and excessive lubrication can cause damage to motors and paintwork, and will seep out of the model into packing material when the model is in storage.

WHEEL CLEANING

The subject of cleaning locomotive wheels has been touched upon earlier (see Chapter 3), but this is an essential part of cleaning and maintaining the locomotive fleet. Examining the wheels of locomotives and rolling stock shows how much dirt gets picked up during normal operation. Rolling stock wheels build up a layer of grime too that can, in the finer scales, actually cause derailments as the effect of a finer flange is further reduced by dirt. Dirt is usually collected from the rails and may include dust that has fallen onto the layout during construction and modelling phases. The use of dustsheets can dramatically reduce the 'dirt' that comes into contact with the layout and reduces dirty wheel problems. Consider using fibreglass scratch pencils to gently scour dirt away while the wheels rotate or a device such as the Kadee 'Speedy' wheel cleaner.

A useful technique employed by modellers on certain locomotives that would otherwise be awkward to clean, such as those with extended cranks and outside frame coupling rods, is to place a few drops of IPA on a lint-free cloth or kitchen towel, place it over a piece of track and then to run the locomotive partly on the cloth and partly on the track so it picks up power. The dirt is easily removed as the wheels rotate on the cloth. To ensure all the wheels are properly cleaned, the locomotive is turned round and the task repeated.

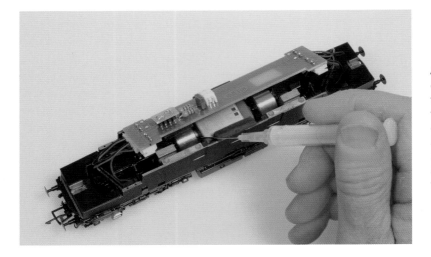

Motor bearings can become dry after a period of storage, owing to a lack of use or simply due to time. Motor bearings can make a squealing noise that sounds like the model is destroying itself! A tiny drop of oil on motor shaft bearings will cure the problem.

Sparingly lubricate bearings and flexible couplings on drive shafts. Don't forget the motor bearings too.

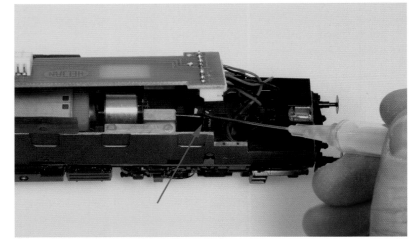

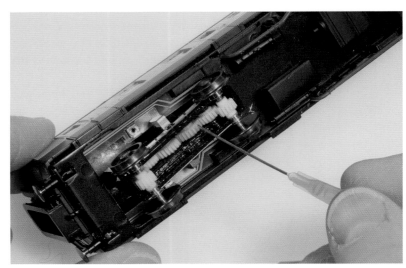

Bogie gears need to be lubricated as well. This picture shows oil being applied with a small, specially adapted syringe.

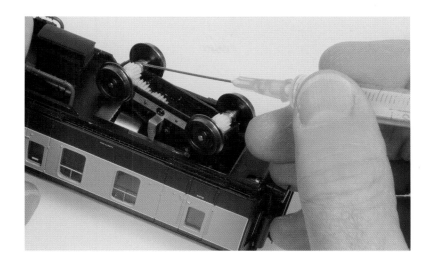

Do not apply oil directly from a bottle and avoid household oils such as 3-in-1 oil, which is too heavy for this application. Fine model oil or clock oil will do the job well. Apply sparingly with a cocktail stick, syringe or even a pin. Don't forget to apply oil to axle bearings.

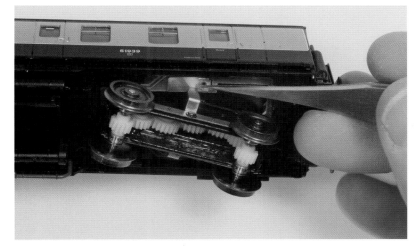

Check electrical contacts within the model for tarnish, fluff and dirt, all of which could prevent the efficient conductivity of electricity to the motor.

Stray fluff and pet hairs can get into wheel bearings and mechanisms, causing unwanted and undesirable binding. Carefully remove it with tweezers.

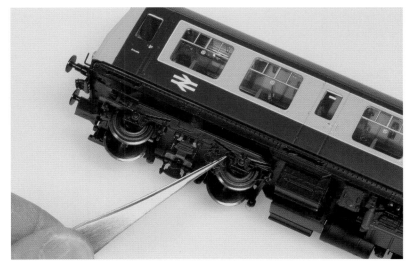

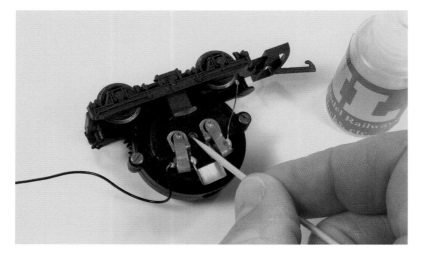

A squealing noise from ringfield motors indicates that the spindle bearings are dry. Use a cocktail stick to apply a small drop of oil directly to the bearing.

Do not forget the spindle bearing on the reverse side and some grease to the gears too.

Inspect carbon brushes by carefully bending back the spring cover and extracting the spring and brush with tweezers.

DUSTING AND CLEANING THE BODYSHELL

Another case for using dustsheets to cover a layout when not in use is the amount of dust that can build up on the surface of models over time. Ultimately, dust does little for their appearance, shows up dramatically in photographs and can be awkward to clean away from models with complex shapes and corners, such as steam locomotives. It is useful to have a clean one-inch paintbrush with soft bristles for the task of dusting models. A brush will get into tight corners without tearing off delicate detail. It's a technique I find to be safer than using a vacuum cleaner to remove dust.

Fingerprints are another undesirable on the surface of models, as are grease and oil. These should be carefully removed with a clean cloth with a tiny amount of IPA if the marks are stubborn. Remember that IPA can remove paint and varnish, particularly acrylic type paints, so only use as a last resort.

CLEANING THE MECHANISM

As seen in the accompanying photographs of the green diesel shunter, grease applied at the factory when the model was built can dry out, becoming hard and unpleasantly troublesome. In this event, the gear towers and drive shafts should be stripped down and the parts carefully cleaned with IPA before reassembly. Before running the model under power, lightly lubricate the parts with fresh grease applied to worm gears and flexible couplings. Fine oils are suitable for final drive gears, axle bushes and motor shaft bearings. Hob-e-Lube offers a gear oil that is thicker than usual and designed for the worm gear at the top of gear towers. It is also very useful for deadening gear noise – don't use toothpaste for this task!

All of the maintenance tips and techniques described in this chapter apply to model steam locomotives as well as to diesels and electric locomotives.

WHEN THINGS GO WRONG

You will be pleased to hear that spares can be found when things break or wear out. Almost anything can be found to be in need of replacement on older models due to wear and tear, including such items as traction tyres, carbon brushes and even complete motors. The major manufacturers are pretty good at making common spares available through stockists, so these should be your first port of call for spares. Alternatively, consider buying up old models for stripping to keep your spares box topped up with the important ones.

Sometimes an accident or serious breakdown means the model needs more than a routine repair.

The green Class 08 shunter featured in this chapter is a prime example. It was acquired as a 'spares or repair' candidate having suffered some abuse. A broken coupling rod was the least of it; it turned out to have chewed gears that needed replacing. These were found at a Hornby spares stockist and ordered online, enabling the model to be put back into traffic. Reference to Hornby's service sheets, which are also available online, helped identify the necessary parts using the model's reference number to ensure I was looking at the code numbers for that release. This is an important factor because model specifications can change. Although a part may look as if it fits, it might have a slight difference making it unworkable, so be alert to such variations.

The older your models, the greater the attention they may need. It's little different for heritage Hastings line 'Thumper' No. 1001. No. 1001 is shedded at St Leonards and beautifully maintained together with a collection of various trailers and a Class 07 shunter by Hastings Diesels Ltd. It has mainline running certification, modern driver safety appliances, and central door locking. Yet without the dedicated restoration and maintenance work undertaken by Hastings Diesels at St Leonards (Hastings), this wonderful heritage DEMU would not be gracing the mainline today.

Damage to models can be physical following a tumble from the layout: losses may include buffers (search the floor for them), glazing inserts, which are likely to be inside the body, broken parts or a split bodyshell. Replacements can usually be located. Internally, the biggest cause of failure is ballast getting into gear towers. Ballast based on rock granules, as sold by some model shops, can do a lot of damage. Synthetic ballast, which is softer, is less likely to create havoc with your prized models.

As demonstrated by the green shunter model, it is possible to buy derelict models and rebuild them quite economically. Simple workbench tools such as tweezers, pliers, soldering iron and jewellers' screwdrivers, both slotted and crosshead, are useful to have to hand. Make use of storage boxes to hold the parts while working on the model and make full use of the information on cleaning and lubrication given

previously. I am aware of a number of modellers who buy up cheap damaged models and successfully make one good one out of two 'demics'. It takes a little knowledge of the structure of the various models to take advantage of this little-known area of railway modelling.

KEEPING RECORDS, BOXES AND INSTRUCTION LEAFLETS

The simplest way of making sure you have everything you might need is to keep all the stuff your model was shipped in, including the instruction leaflets. These are excellent sources of information on how models are constructed and how the bodyshell is secured to the chassis. Some will have a record serial number for reference in case it is necessary to return it for repair under warranty. More important is to make

We have come across this little shunting engine earlier. It was given to me as a 'spares or repair' case with broken coupling rods. The motor worked well, but there was another problem beyond the broken coupling rods that did not become apparent until the rods were replaced and the model tested, as this series of photographs demonstrates.

When there's trouble with a model, locating spare parts is important. Once the broken coupling rods were identified as a symptom, not a cause, of the model's ailments, further investigation was called for. It was traced to damaged gears in the gear tower, as indicated by the red arrow (the wheels removed for access).

This picture shows the main components of the chassis under repair. Note that some fittings can be hidden behind ballast weight attached to the main frames: (A) motor; (B) single flywheel; (C) additional chassis block fixed to the main frames; (D) gear tower spindles.

The additional chassis block was removed to gain access to the worm gear and the top of the gear tower.

The top of the chassis was removed and the worm drive gear also removed for cleaning of grease. This was done with a lint-free cloth and IPA.

The gears were released from the chassis frame by pushing out the gear spindles.

Gears, together with nasty-looking grease, were recovered for inspection and replacement. New gears from a spares dealer were fitted and the spindles refitted.

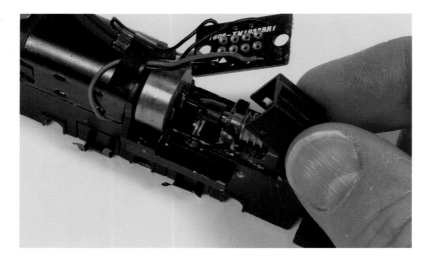

With all the mess cleaned away, the worm gear and retaining clip were reinstated and the chassis tested to see that the new gears were correctly fitted. Light lubrication was also undertaken.

and retain simple records of each locomotive in your fleet. Details could include the type of decoder installed (if using DCC), the address, the locomotive number, brand, when purchased and any problems encountered with it. Some models respond better to one type of lubricant, others may work better with a different brand, so recording such preferences is useful. Another useful tip for DCC-users would be to apply a label with the model's decoder address to the underside of the model or, with the body removed, to the chassis so it can be easily identified.

CONCLUSION

When train services become hesitant on your model railway, the fault may be as simple as dirt or fluff – nothing more than that. There may not be an actual fault with the model itself. However, never forget that models are usually covered by a warranty and if the cleaning and checking of track, connections, wheels and so on brings no satisfactory result, you can always return the model to the retailer for repair. Always keep purchase receipts and be prepared to send models back to the manufacturer in some cases. It is hoped, however, that the techniques in this manual of practical model maintenance and fine tuning will produce lasting results, a reliable railway and much enjoyment of what must be one of the most fascinating of hobbies.

A close-up of the recovered gears shows the damage, which may have been caused by hard material such as rock ballast getting into the mechanism. The red arrows show where the gear teeth have become chewed by grains of foreign material.

Remember: regular inspection and light maintenance will produce reliable and smooth performance on your layout. Keep on top of cleaning and maintenance to keep your fleet in tip-top condition to equal that of this preserved steam locomotive on the Great Central Railway.

USEFUL ADDRESSES

Diesel and electric locomotive nameplates in OO and N gauge (4mm and 2mm scales)

Shawplan Models
2 Upper Dunstead Road
Langley Mill
Nottingham
NG16 4GR

Tel: 01773 718648
www.shawplan.com

Steam locomotive nameplates

CGW Nameplates
Plas Cadfor
Llwyngwril
Gwynedd
LL37 2LA

Tel: 01341 250407

Steam locomotive and BR blue era diesel locomotive nameplates

Modelmaster Professional/Jackson Evans
31 Crown Street
Ayr
KA8 8AG

Tel: 01292 289770
www.modelmasterdecals.com

Replacement wheels and conversion packs

Gear Services (Letchworth) Ltd
Unit 25
Such Close II Industrial Estate
Letchworth Garden City
Hertfordshire
SG6 1JF

Tel: 01462 681007
Fax: 01462 681577
www.ultrascale.co.uk

Materials and tools for maintenance and cleaning

Nairnshire Modelling Supplies
PO Box 6078
Nairn
Nairnshire
IV12 5LF

Tel: 01667 451130
www.nairnshire-modelling-supplies.co.uk